ENGLISH PAPER MONEY

Vincent Duggleby

(Edited by Colin Narbeth)

Stanley Gibbons Publications Ltd
399 Strand, London WC2R 0LX

By Appointment to Her Majesty The Queen
Stanley Gibbons Ltd, London Philatelists

© Stanley Gibbons Publications Ltd 1984

First published 1975
Second edition 1980
Third edition 1984

ISBN 0 85259 083 0

G117328

Item No. 2822

Phototypeset by Input Typesetting Ltd, London

Printed in Great Britain by
Garden City Press, Letchworth

Contents

Preface to the Third Edition

It is now more than ten years since the first edition of *English Paper Money* was put in hand, and since then there has been a dramatic increase in the number of banknote collectors, or notaphilists as they are sometimes known. Since the second edition of the book was published in 1980, further research has extended the range of serial prefixes and new information has come to light, most notably details of the unissued "second series" banknotes designed by Stephen Gooden; not that the story is by any means complete, nor will it be so long as paper money remains the primary medium of exchange and measure of value.

Since 1980 the world has experienced a recession of unprecedented severity; at the same time inflation has been reined back and so paper money is no longer losing its purchasing power in Britain at such an alarming rate. The effect on many areas of collecting has been a sharp fall in prices from 1980–1983 and only recently has the market begun to stabilise. Banknotes were no exception. This is not to say ALL notes fell in value, but collectors became much more discerning, underlining the importance of condition in all modern notes, though there will always be rarities (such as 19th century Bank of England notes) which will be snapped up regardless.

Meanwhile the present Chief Cashier of the Bank of England, Mr David Somerset, has completed four years in office. During this period a £50 note has been added to the Pictorial "Series D" notes, and the £1 note is under threat of extinction in the near future despite evident public hostility towards the £1 coin which appeared in April 1983. Whether the UK mainland will follow the Isle of Man into plastic money remains to be seen.

Whatever happens, English banknotes will remain eminently collectable, and it is still possible to start by looking at the contents of your wallet or handbag. You will find various different prefixes and you may find an AO1 or O1A note which are those most sought after by collectors (preferably in mint condition). From time to time the Bank of England issue experimental notes. The celebrated "R" (research) £1 note of O'Brien is a case in point. More recently a series of £5 Somerset notes came out to help in Optical Character Recognition; these "OCR" notes carry the special serial prefix number 91. It may be possible to persuade the manager of your local bank to let you examine any bundles of old notes that are paid in before they are returned to the Bank of England for destruction. Although notes may lose their legal tender status, they are always redeemable £ for £ against new notes. . . "I promise to pay the bearer on demand", as the legend goes.

All prefix codes are listed in this catalogue, and the new collector will find additional general information at the end of the book, including a special section on the old white high-denomination notes. Established collectors will recognise one important change to the numbering of the early Bank of England issues. Instead of allocating a number to every individual note, they are now listed under a "collective" number for each cashier. So few of these notes have survived that most collectors will be pleased to have a single example from any Chief Cashier prior to J. G. Nairne. Apart from that the original classification remains unchanged in this third edition and your guide to the fascinating world of English Paper Money.

London   VINCENT DUGGLEBY

Copyright B.B.C.

The Author

Vincent Duggleby is recognised as the leading authority on British Treasury and Bank of England notes of the twentieth century. His research has brought to light many aspects of note design and productions—particularly during the First World War—which were previously unknown, and his widely circulated charts of the Bank of England prefix system (first published in *Coins, Stamps and Collecting* in 1971) are regarded as a standard reference.

Educated at Blundell's School, Devon and Worcester College, Oxford, he is now Financial Editor of B.B.C. Radio.

He has been a member of the International Bank Note Society since 1969, and he is also a Fellow of the Royal Philatelic Society, London—specialising in the stamps of the island of St. Vincent.

Acknowledgements

The author expresses his thanks to the following organisations for assistance given during the compilation of this book:
The Inland Revenue (particularly the Director of Stamping).
The Public Record Office.
The British Museum.
H.M. Treasury.
The Bank of England (who have kindly sanctioned publication).
It would be impossible to list all those individuals who have helped in some way with new information since the first edition appeared but mention should be made of the help and advice given by David Keable, George Webb, Howard Lunn, Colin Narbeth and Yasha Beresiner.
David Keable in particular has played a major part in the repricing of this third edition.

Catalogue Terms

Obverse

Front of a banknote.

Reverse

Back of a banknote.

Prefix

The combination of letters and numbers that precede the actual serial number, e.g. on Bank of England notes:
X41 (= letter, number, number)
28A (= number, number, letter)
R31L (= letter, number, number, letter)
AN64 (= letter, letter, number, number)
On Treasury notes the prefixes most usually found are:
$\frac{B}{41}$ (= letter over number)

$\frac{H2}{23}$ (= letter and figure over number)

Dot

A variety found on some Treasury notes where the prefix "No" has a full stop after or under it. In some cases this is normal, in others it is a variety.

Dash

As above but a dash instead of a full stop. This may also be referred to as a "square dot" variety.

Metal thread

The "thread" or metal filament inserted into the paper of modern Bank of England notes which shows up clearly when the note is held up to the light.

Illustrations

Illustrations of single notes in this catalogue are approximately ½ linear size.

Colours of notes

Generally only the predominant colours are given in the lists.

Prices

Banknotes have been priced for Very Fine (VF) condition to 1914 and thereafter for Very Fine and Extremely Fine (EF) conditions. They are available with or without specified serial prefix. It should be remembered that many of them can be obtained for very much less in worn condition; 100% uncirculated notes cost more. For information on how to grade condition *see* page 160.

In the price columns:
– Exists but no price can be quoted.
* Not yet identified, so no price can be quoted.
† Readily obtained from circulation.

Treasury Notes

The outbreak of the First World War in August 1914 proved to be the end of Britain's "Golden Age" in more ways than one. Up until that time the gold sovereign and half-sovereign had circulated as everyday currency for nearly a century, although the ordinary working man might well never handle them.

Following the 1833 Bank Act, Bank of England notes were legal tender in England and Wales only for amounts of £5 and above. With the passing of the Currency and Bank Notes Act on 5 August 1914 (the day after war was declared), the Treasury was empowered to issue currency notes of £1 and 10s. with full legal tender status, and indirect gold convertibility through the Bank of England. The Bank, anticipating the inevitability of war and restrictions on gold, had in fact already been working behind the scenes. A traditional design for a £1 Bank of England note had been prepared (see page 66), but it was never formally presented.

Instead H.M. Treasury, helped by the Inland Revenue, rushed through an emergency design during the weekend of 1/2 August, and the notes were printed in round-the-clock shifts by Waterlow Bros. and Layton, with help on the 10s. note by De La Rue. The Bank Holiday was extended for three days, and minutes in the Public Record Office give a graphic description of the wrangle between the Chancellor of the Exchequer, Lloyd George, and the city bankers over the status of the new notes. Lloyd George was careful not to reveal his hand until it was virtually a *fait accompli*, and only conceded a major point on convertibility, that without it the notes would certainly go to a discount.

The first Treasury notes were hurriedly and badly designed, and since there was no supply of banknote paper available (other than that held by the Bank), the printers had to use postage stamp paper, bearing the Royal Cypher ("Simple") watermark. The notes were signed by the Permanent Secretary to the Treasury, Sir John Bradbury, and measured 5 by 2½ in. The £1 was issued on 7 August and the 10s. came out a week later, and both quickly acquired the nickname of "Bradburys".

It was only a matter of days before plans were put in hand to produce a more considered and permanent design. Despite strong and colourful competition from the various printers (Bradbury Wilkinson were particularly pressing), the contract for the second issue was again divided between De La Rue (£1 and 10s.), and Waterlow Bros. and Layton (10s. only). The designs were those of Mr. George Eve who also designed some of the George V stamps. On 28 August 1914 they were approved by Lloyd George who remarked during the second reading of the Currency and Banknotes Amendment Bill the previous day that: "The new design will not compare in artistic merit with that of the Scottish Banks. We had to consider a good many things and the first thing to consider in a note is whether it is easily forgeable or not. If you have a good mass of colour on your note it is not so easy to detect forgery. The simpler a design is the more difficult it is to forge, just as the simpler a signature is the more difficult it is to forge. Signatures with great flourishes are most easily forged. If you have a simple signature like that on the Bank of England note, it is the most difficult thing in the world for the forger. It is much more difficult to imitate simplicity than it is to imitate flourishes and special adornments. That is the principle on which we have proceeded in the preparation of these notes. . ."

A rather different view was taken (in private) by the Chairman of the Board of Inland Revenue, Sir Matthew Nathan: "The design is not a good one (I preferred the school leaving certificate) but I think we shall get a clear well printed note with easily seen and distinctive water-mark, making forgeries difficult. There will be no undue delay and the cost will not be excessive. When the public abuses the design we will take refuge in it having been made by H.M.'s designer of stamps." The new £1 note duly appeared on 23 October 1914 and the 10s. note on 21 January 1915 without any noticeable complaint!

It was, however, only a few months before discussions were under way on yet another change, adopting many of the principles which had just been rejected. Preliminary work on the third issue notes was undertaken by a designer known only as "Carlton", whose background and credentials remain a mystery. There is, unfortunately, a gap in the archives and the next thing we know is that in March 1916 Bertram Mackennal (designer of the coinage) had been "good enough to step into the breach".

The main difference in the Mackennal design is, in fact, in the portrait of the King—could the original have met with Royal disapproval? The progressive proof illustrations (*see* page 35) show similar vignettes of St. George and the Dragon, based on the model by Pistrucci, used on the sovereign and on various crowns. The new £1 notes were printed by Waterlow Bros. and Layton despite an attempt by De La Rue to claim breach of contract by the Government. *The Times* commented: "In design it is an entire departure from the old which as an artistic production it leaves far behind . . . the most distinctive feature of the note is the splendid likeness of the King on the right hand, which on first glance appears to be embossed owing to the blending of its green and brown . . . cases have come to light of the imitation of the old issue; it is doubtful whether even the most expert artist in forgery could reproduce the new. On the back is a coloured picture of the Houses of Parliament. This is intended as a further safeguard against the note being inadvertently thrown into the wastepaper basket or otherwise destroyed as a useless piece of paper. . ." The £1 was issued on 22 February 1917 and the 10s. notes, with a vignette of Britannia standing, on 22 October 1918.

It was around this time that serious concern was being felt over the shortage of silver coinage, mainly due to inflation and hoarding, and there were proposals to remedy this by the issue of 5s. notes. Bradbury himself was doubtful and the Bank totally opposed: "If 5s. notes are put into circulation it will very soon become necessary to print notes for smaller denominations" they claimed. Nonetheless the Government pressed ahead with the required bill, and were only dissuaded at the very last minute from introducing it on 19 July 1918. Matters did not, however, rest there. The 5s. notes had already been prepared, and by the end of the year designs for the 2s. 6d. and 1s. were also in hand.

On 27 August 1919 Sir John Bradbury left the Treasury to become Principal British Delegate to the Reparation Commission and was succeeded by Sir Warren Fisher (formerly Chairman of the Board of Inland Revenue). Fisher viewed the currency notes "with a certain temperamental disinclination" but concluded in his memorandum to the Chancellor, Mr. Austen Chamberlain, that they should still bear the signature of the Secretary to the Treasury. "My signature" he added "will need some compression!"

There were no more major changes to Treasury notes, although a new style watermark was incorporated into the £1 in 1923 and, following the Royal and Parliamentary Titles Act of 1927, the heading of the notes was changed to "United Kingdom of Great Britain and *Northern* Ireland". More important was the authorisation on 31 October 1919 "for the printing of 10 million notes of the approved design and bearing the signature of Sir N. F. Warren Fisher in each of the denominations 5s., 2s. 6d. and 1s.". Ten days later the First World War ended and the notes were never needed.

Further information on Treasury notes will be found in an article by the author published in the *International Bank Note Society Journal* Vol. 20, No. 2 (1981).

JOHN BRADBURY (FIRST BARON BRADBURY) (1872–1950)

Entered the Civil Service in 1896, first the Colonial Office and then the Treasury. After serving under Asquith and then Lloyd George (including help with the famous Budget of 1909). Bradbury was appointed one of two permanent Secretaries of the Treasury in 1913 along with Sir Thomas Heath. On the outbreak of the First World War. Bradbury quickly realised the necessity of replacing gold with paper currency, and the banknotes which were issued carried his signature; they were immediately nicknamed "Bradburys". He remained the Government's chief financial adviser during the War, eventually leaving the Treasury on 27 August 1919 to become principal British delegate to the Reparation Commission. He was knighted in 1913 and created a peer in January 1925.

First Issue

1914 (7 August) ONE POUND

Emergency issue authorised by H.M. Government and designed at the Royal Mint. Surface-printed in sheets of 36 (4 × 9) on one side only by

BRADBURY *(contd.)*

Waterlow Bros. and Layton from plates by Eyre and Spottiswoode, on ordinary stamp paper with watermark of the Royal Cypher ("Simple") and the word or part of the word POSTAGE. First-issue Treasury notes measure 127 × 63·5 mm (5 × 2½ in.) and were legal tender until 12 June 1920. The first two and a half million notes, which were delivered to the banks on Thursday, 6 August, for issue the following morning, can be identified by the large capital A, B or C prefix (*see* T1 and T2).

			Price	
			EF	VF
T1	£1	Black on white *Prefix coding:* Single capital letter and six-digit serial number. *Quantity printed:* 2½ million. *Serial letters:* A, B and C.	£650	£450
T2	£1	Black on white As T1 but with the full stop omitted after serial letter. *Serial letters:* A, B and C.	£650	£450

T1 (and its variety T2) can rightly be described as the "first modern British banknotes".

T3	£1	Black on white *Prefix coding:* Letter over number ("dot") with		
		Type 1: Four digits	from	£750
		Type 2: Five digits	£450	£285
		Type 3: Six digits	£375	£250
		A variant of this note has the six digits *in a smaller typeface similar to T5.*		
		Type 4: Seven digits	from	£750
		Quantity printed: Not known. *Serial letters:* A to Z (probably not inclusive)		

T4	£1	Black on white
		Prefix coding: Letter over number
		    ("dash")
		    with		

		Type 1: Four digits	from	£750
		Type 2: Five digits	£450	£285
		Type 3: Six digits ⎱ Not yet seen	–	–
		Type 4: Seven digits ⎰	–	–

Price
EF   VF

Quantity printed: Not known.
Serial letters:
   A to Z (not inclusive)

T5   £1   Black on white
Prefix coding: Letter over number ("dot"
   or "dash") but the digits set in much
   smaller type.

		EF	VF
Type 1: Four digits	Not yet seen	–	–
Type 2: Five digits		–	–
Type 3: Six digits ("dash")		£675	£450
Type 4: Seven digits ("dot")		from £750	

Quantity printed: Not known.
Serial letters:
   B, D (and probably others).

T6   £1   Black on white
Prefix coding: Double letter over
   number ("dot") with six digits.
Quantity printed: Not known.
Serial letters:
   BB, CC, DD, HH, JJ, LL (and   £675   £450
   probably others)

T7   £1   Black on white
Prefix coding: Double letter over
   number ("dot" placed after No.) and
   four digits.
Quantity printed: Not known.
Serial letters:
   LL (and possibly others)   from £1000

Due to the practice of printing some additional notes down the sheet margin (*see* illustration on page 7) most of the above can be found with watermark sideways. The watermark is also found inverted and sideways inverted. These varieties are rare, and likely to command a premium.

Note—First issue Treasury £1 notes with four digits are now thought to be replacements, although the general inconsistency of the system makes it possible other methods were used to replace faulty notes. Some people have questioned the possibility that notes with five digits were printed by De La Rue. There is no evidence to support this, though bundles of printed notes might have been sent to them for numbering only.

BRADBURY (contd.)

T1

The following illutrations of typefaces T2 and T7 have been reproduced from actual notes to facilitate identification:

A.476039

Type 1

$^{L}_{36}$ N⁰ 0012

Type 4/1

A 040564

Type 2

$^{L}_{7}$ N⁰ 21787

Type 4/2

$^{G}_{13}$ N⁰ 1791

Type 3/1

$^{D}_{8}$ N⁰ 002359

Type 5/3

$^{B}_{32}$ N⁰ 11955

Type 3/2

$^{B}_{13}$ N⁰ 0034287

Type 5/4

$^{A}_{29}$ N⁰ 015437

Type 3/3

$^{LL}_{34}$ N⁰ 000299

Type 6

$^{B}_{40}$ N⁰ 0071006

Type 3/4

$^{LL}_{34}$ NO. 0300

Type 7

Additional notes printed at edge of sheet of First Issue £1

1914 (14 August) TEN SHILLINGS

Emergency issue authorised by H.M. Government and designed at the Royal Mint. Surface-printed in sheets of 36 (4 × 9) on one side only by Waterlow Bros. and Layton (T8 and T9) and by De La Rue and Co. (T10) on ordinary stamp paper as the £1 above. Dimensions and legal tender also as £1 above.

			Price	
			EF	*VF*
T8	**10s.**	Red on white (Waterlow)	£525	£300
		Prefix coding: Letter over number ("dot") and six digits.		
		Quantity printed: Not known.		
		Serial letters:		
		S and T (and possibly others)		

BRADBURY (contd.)

Price

EF   *VF*

T9   10s. Red on white (Waterlow).   £350   £225
As T8 but the word "No" is set in
different type and precedes the
prefix coding.
Quantity printed: Not known.
Serial letter:
A

T10   10s. Red on white (De La Rue)   £525   £300
Prefix coding: Letter over number
("dot") and five digits.
Quantity printed: Not known.
Serial letters:
A to Z (not inclusive)

As with the £1 some additional notes were printed in the sheet margin
and the above can be found with watermark sideways, inverted, and
sideways inverted.

All varieties are rare.

The following illustrations of typefaces T8 to T10 have been reproduced
from actual notes to facilitate identification:

$^{S}_{25}$ N⁰ 058890

Type 8

№ ✝205949

Type 9

$^{C}_{10}$ N⁰ 08991

Type 10

T9

Sheet of First Issue 10s

Second Issue

1914 (23 October) ONE POUND

Designed by George Eve. Surface-printed in sheets of 30 (5 × 6) on one side only by De La Rue and Co. on banknote paper manufactured by William Joynson and Co. with watermark of wavy lines incorporating the Royal Cypher, the ONE POUND denomination and the four British emblems:

T11 Type 2

BRADBURY (contd.)

rose, thistle, shamrock and daffodil. Second-issue Treasury £1 notes measure 149 × 85 mm (5⅞ × 3¼ in.) and were legal tender until 12 June 1920.

			Price	
			EF	*VF*
T11	£1	Black on white		
		Prefix coding:		
		Type 1: Letter over number and five digits	£165	£95
		Type 2: Letter and figure "1" over number and five digits	£185	£125
		Quantity printed: Not known.		
		Serial letters:		
		A to Z (probably not inclusive)		
		A1 to L1 (possibly not inclusive)		

1915 (21 January) TEN SHILLINGS

Designed by George Eve. Surface-printed in sheets of 30 (5 × 6) on one side only by De La Rue and Co. (T12) and by Waterlow Bros. and Layton (T13) on banknote paper manufactured by William Joynson and Co. as the £1 above. Second-issue Treasury 10s. notes measure 136 × 76 mm (5⅜ × 3 in.) and were legal tender until 12 June 1920.

T12	10s.	Red on white (shades)		
		Prefix coding:		
		Type 1: Letter over number and five digits.	£125	70.00
		Type 2: Letter and figure "1" over number and five digits	£125	70.00
		Type 3: Letter and figure "2" over number and five digits	£165	95.00
		Quantity printed: Not known.		
		Serial letters:		
		A to M (probably not inclusive)		
		A1 to Z1 (probably not inclusive)		
		A2 to C2		

T13	10s.	Red on white (shades)		
		Prefix coding:		
		Type 1: Letter over number and six digits	£150	85.00
		Type 2: Letter and figure "1" over number and six digits	£150	85.00
		Quantity printed: Not known.		
		Serial letters:		
		N to Z (probably not inclusive)		
		Q1 to Z1 (probably not inclusive)		

T12 Type 3

T13 Type 1

A most interesting proof (in black) of the second issue 10s. shows the endorsement of the Inland Revenue's Director of Stamping, Harry Birtles, 22 December 1914 and is illustrated above.

BRADBURY (contd.)

The Dardanelles Campaign Overprints

Despite extensive research little of real substance has been found relating to the use of these rare and fascinating notes. The official Treasury minute in the Public Record Office states that the £1 and 10s. currency notes were issued for use by the entire British Military Expeditionary Forces in the Mediterranean and the Naval Expeditionary Forces from May–June 1915. Supplies of the notes were supposedly sent to Malta and Alexandria, but whether these were the Gallipoli overprints, or when and for how long they were issued is still in dispute.

The student will find further information and conjecture in two articles by Fred Philipson in the *International Bank Note Society Journal* Vol. 10, No. 4, 1971; and Vol. 15, No. 4, 1976. Another useful article by Samuel Lachman appears in Vol. 15, No. 3, 1976.

According to the Inland Revenue logbook the notes were actually overprinted on 21 May 1915. The translation of the Arabic characters on the £1 (T14) reads: "Piastres silver 120" on the top line and "Piastres silver one hundred and twenty" on the bottom. The overprint on the 10s. (T15) reads: "Piastres silver 60" and "Piastres silver sixty" respectively.

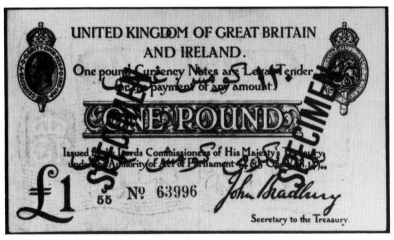

T14

			Price	
			EF	*VF*
T14	£1	Black on white (red overprint)	from £2500	£1250

Prefix coding: Letter over number (as T11).
Quantity overprinted: Not known.
Serial letters:
F, J, M, Y (and possibly others)

	Price	
	EF	*VF*

T15 **10s.**   Red on white (black overprint)   £475   £225
      Prefix coding:
         Letter over number six digits (as
         T13).
      Serial letters:
         Y and Z.

T15

Third Issue

1917 (22 January) ONE POUND

Designed by Bertram Mackennal. Vignette of St. George and the Dragon
based on the work of Benedetto Pistrucci for the Royal Mint. Photogravure-
printed in sheets of 21 (3 × 7) by Waterlow Bros. and Layton on banknote
paper manufactured by William Joynson and Co. with multiple watermark
of Vandyck (diagonal) lines incorporating the Royal Cypher, the denomination ONE POUND and the four British emblems. Third-issue Treasury £1
notes measure 151 × 84 mm ($5^{15}/_{16}$ × $3^5/_{16}$ in.) and were legal tender until
1 August 1933.

T16   **£1**   Brown, purple and green (shades) on
           white or cream
        Prefix coding: Letter over number.
        Quantity printed: 825 million.
        Serial letters:

A		65.00	35.00
B, C, D, E, F, G, H	*each*	45.00	25.00
Z		60.00	32.00

BRADBURY (contd.)

Sheet of T15

T16 showing dot

Common reverse of Third and Fourth Issue £1

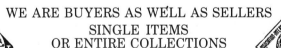

BRADBURY (contd.)

Bradbury and Fisher £1 notes carrying the serial "Z" are from the bottom right-hand corner of the sheet, giving a ratio of 20 to 1. It is thought that these "Z" notes may have been used for control purposes.

1918 (22 October) TEN SHILLINGS

Designed by Bertram Mackennal. Photogravure-printed in sheets of 20 (4 × 5) by Waterlow Bros. and Layton on banknote paper manufactured by William Joynson and Co. with composite watermark incorporating the Royal Cypher, the denomination TEN SHILLINGS at the top and the four British emblems. Third-issue 10s. notes measures 138 × 78 mm (5⁷/₁₆ × 3¹/₁₆ in.) and were legal tender until 1 August 1933. The serial numbers printed in BLACK.

			Price	
			EF	VF
T17	**10s.**	Green, purple and brown on white *Prefix coding:* Letter over number (black "dot"). *Quantity printed:* 100 million. *Serial letter:* A	£285	£165
T18	**10s.**	Green, purple and brown on white *Prefix-coding:* Letter over number (black "dash"). *Quantity printed:* Included in T17 above. *Serial letter:* As in T17 above	£250	£145

T18 showing dash

1918 (16 December) TEN SHILLINGS

As last issue, but serial number is printed in RED.

Common reverse of Third and Fourth Issue 10s.

		Price	
		EF	*VF*

T19 **10s.** Green, purple and brown on white
Prefix coding: Letter over number (red "dot").
Quantity printed: 120 million.
Serial letters:
B, C.   from £425

T20 **10s.** Green, purple and brown on white
Prefix coding: Letter over number (red "dash" or "square dot").
Quantity printed: included in T19 above.
Serial letters:
As in T19 above   £185   £115

1917 (1 December) Five Shillings

Ratified (i.e. approved for distribution) 21 February 1918. Designed by Bertram Mackennal. Photogravure printed in sheets of 35 (5 × 7) by Waterlow Bros. and Layton on banknote paper manufactured by William Joynson and Co. with composite watermark incorporating the Royal Cypher and the denomination five shillings. Treasury 5s. notes, signed by John Bradbury, measure 127 × 76 mm (5 × 3 in.) and were distributed to the clearing banks in Great Britain and Ireland, but were not issued to the public. The notes were destroyed in November 1919.

                                                VF

T21 **5s.** Deep violet and green on white
Prefix coding: Not known.
Quantity printed: 7·9 million.
Serial letters:
Not known   from £2500

BRADBURY (contd.)

T21 proof

1918 (November) HALF-CROWN

Designed by C. Howard with vignette of King George V by T. S. Harrison. Although proofs were prepared by De La Rue and Co., there was no production run of Treasury 2s. 6d. notes signed by John Bradbury.

Price
VF

T22 **2s.6d.** Olive-green and chocolate on white
            Prefix coding: Not known.
            Quantity printed: None.
            Serial letter:
                    A   from £2500
    Note—A specimen note is known with the serial $\frac{A}{1}$ 000000

1918 (November) ONE SHILLING

Designed by C. Howard with vignette of King George V by T. S. Harrison. Although proofs were prepared by De La Rue and Co., there was no production run of Treasury 1s. notes signed by John Bradbury.

Price
EF   VF

T23 **1s.**   Green and brown on white   –   –
            Prefix coding: Not known.
            Quantity printed: None.
            Serial letters:
                Not allocated.

SIR (NORMAN FENWICK) WARREN FISHER (1879–1948)

Entered the Civil Service in 1903 and was posted to Inland Revenue department, where he became private secretary to the Chairman of the Board, Robert Chalmers, in 1907. After moving for a short time to the National Health Insurance Commission for England in 1912, he returned the following year to Somerset House as a Commissioner of Inland Revenue. He was appointed Deputy Chairman of the Board in October 1914 and Chairman in August 1918. On 1 October 1919 Warren Fisher went to the Treasury as Permanent Secretary where he stayed until his retirement in 1939. He received a knighthood in 1919. Treasury notes signed by Fisher were of the same design as those of the Third Issue signed by Bradbury.

Sheet of T21

First Issue

1919 (30 September) ONE POUND

Design, watermark and dimensions as Bradbury T16 above. Photogravure-printed in sheets of 21 (3 × 7) by Waterlow Bros. and Layton on banknote paper manufactured by William Joynson and Co.

FISHER (contd.)   *Price*

                                       EF   *VF*

T24   **£1**   Brown and green (shades) on white or
              cream
              Prefix coding: Letter over number.
              quantity printed: 1150 million.
              serial letters:

		EF	VF
K, L, M, N, O, P, R, S, T, U, W, X,	*each*	40.00	25.00
Z		48.00	30.00

For notes carrying the serial "Z" *see* under T16 and illustrated sheet.

T24

1919 (30 September) TEN SHILLINGS

Design, watermark and dimensions as Bradbury T19 above. Photogravure-printed in sheets of 20 (4 × 5) by Waterlow Bros. and Layton on banknote paper manufactured by William Joynson and Co.

                                       Price

                                      EF   *VF*

T25   **10s.**   Green, purple and brown on white
              Prefix coding: Letter over number (red
                "dot")
              Quantity printed: 500 million.
              Serial letters:

		EF	VF
D, E, F, G, H	*each*	£125	70.00

T26   **10s.**   Green, purple and brown on white
              Prefix coding: Letter over number (red
                "dash").
              Quantity printed: Included in T25
                above.
              Serial letters:

	EF	VF
As T25 above	90.00	50.00

FISHER (contd.)

Sheet of T24

T26

1919 (28 November) FIVE SHILLINGS

Design, watermark and dimensions as Bradbury T21 above.
Photogravure-printed in sheets of 35 (5 × 7) by Waterlow Bros. and
Layton on banknote paper manufactured by William Joynson and Co.
Although Treasury 5s. notes signed by Fisher were not officially issued
a few found their way into circulation.

Price
VF

T27   **5s.**   Violet and green on white
              Prefix coding: Letter over number.
              Quantity printed: 10 million.
              Serial letter:
                  B   from £2000

T27

Reverse of T27 common to Bradbury and Fisher

1919 (19 November) HALF-CROWN

Designed by C. Howard with vignette of King George V by T. S. Harrison.
Surface-printed in sheets of 40 (4 × 10) by De La Rue and Co. on banknote
paper manufactured by William Joynson and Co. with composite watermark incorporating the Royal Cypher and the denomination HALF-CROWN.
Treasury 2s. 6d. notes measure 117 × 75 mm (4⅝ × 2¹⁵/₁₆ in.) and were
not officially issued. A few, however, found their way into circulation.

FISHER (contd.)

T28

Reverse of T28

Price
VF

T28 **2s.6d.** Olive-green and chocolate on white
      Prefix coding: Letter over number
      Quantity printed: 10 million.
      Serial letter:
            A   from £2000
1919 (19 November) ONE SHILLING

Designed by C. Howard with vignette of King George V by T. S. Harrison.
Surface-printed in sheets of 49 (7 × 7) by De La Rue and Co. on banknote
paper manufactured by William Joynson and Co. with composite
watermark incorporating the Royal Cypher and the denomination ONE
SHILLING. Treasury 1s. notes measure 104 × 66 mm (4⅛ × 2⅝ in.) and
were not officially issued. A few, however, found their way into
circulation.

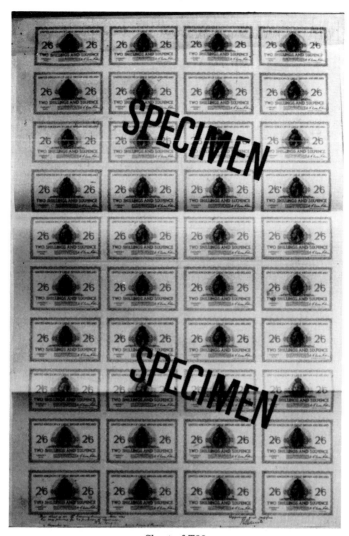

Sheet of T28

Price
VF

T29 **1s.** Green and brown on white
Prefix coding: Letter over number.
Quantity printed: 10 million.
Serial letter:
    B   from £2000

FISHER (contd.)

T29

Reverse of T29

Sheet of T29

Second Issue

1922 (6 November) Ten Shillings

Design, watermark and dimensions at T25 above, but the word "No" is omitted where it precedes the serial number. Photogravure-printed in sheets of 20 (4 × 5) by Waterlow and Sons (who had taken over Waterlow Bros. and Layton in 1920) on banknote paper manufactured by Portals Ltd. (who replaced William Joynson).

				Price	
				EF	VF
T30	**10s.**	Green, purple and brown on white *Prefix coding:* Letter over number ("No" omitted). *Quantity printed:* 900 million. *Serial letters:* J, K, L, M, N, O, P, R, S	*each*	55.00	30.00

T30

1923 (26 February) One Pound

Design and dimensions as T24 above, but watermark is now composite so that the words ONE POUND appear in the top of each note. Photogravure-printed in sheets of 21 (3 × 7) by Waterlow and Sons on banknote paper manufactured by Portals Ltd.

T31	**£1**	Brown and green on white *Prefix coding:* Letter and figure "1" over number ("dot"). *Quantity printed:* 1700 million. *Serial letters:*			
		A1		45.00	26.00
		B1, C1, D1, E1, F1, G1, H1, J1, K1, L1, M1, N1, O1, P1, R1	*each*	35.00	20.00
		Z1		45.00	26.00

For notes carrying the serial "Z" *see* under T16 and illustrated sheet.

FISHER (contd.)

T31

T32 **£1** Brown and green on white
Prefix coding: Letter and figure "1"
over number ("dash").
Quantity printed: Included in T31
above.
Serial letters:
See below   65.00   38.00

Since the dash, or to be more accurate, the square dot, appears on
random notes in particular sheets, it may be found under any serial
letter. Most examples, however, have turned up with H1 and M1 serials.

Third Issue

1927 (25 July) TEN SHILLINGS

Design, watermark and dimensions as T25 above, but following the passing
of the Royal and Parliamentary Titles Act of 1927 into law, the wording
on the notes was altered to read UNITED KINGDOM OF GREAT BRITAIN AND
NORTHERN IRELAND. Photogravure-printed in sheets of 20 (4 × 5) by
Waterlow and Sons.

T33 **10s.** Green, purple and brown on white
Prefix coding: Letter over number
("No" omitted).
Quantity printed: 250 million.
Serial letters:
S, T, U, W   *each*   68.00   40.00

FISHER (contd.)

T33

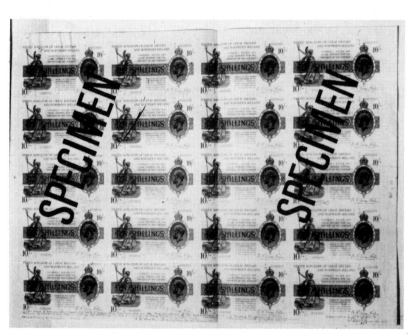

Sheet of T33

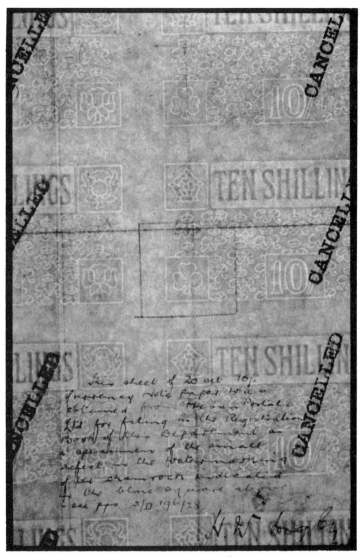

T33 faulty watermark

T33 (faulty watermark)
Some of the notes of this issue have a faulty watermark. The fault, when
it occurs, is on the fourth note of the third row, i.e. notes with serial
prefix numbers 12, 32, 52, 72 and 92. The fault is in a misshapen
shamrock, which is not properly indented on its right-hand side (*see*
illustration).

Price (VF) £200

FISHER (contd.)

1927 (25 July) ONE POUND

Design, watermark and dimensions as T24 above, but wording is altered to read UNITED KINGDOM OF GREAT BRITAIN AND NORTHERN IRELAND. Photogravure-printed in sheets of 21 (3 × 7) by Waterlow and Sons.

				Price	
				EF	*VF*
T34	**£1**	Brown and green on white			
		Prefix coding: Letter and figure "1" over number ("dot").			
		Quantity printed: 530 million.			
		Serial letters:			
		S1, T1, U1, W1, X1	*each*	60.00	35.00
		Z1		68.00	40.00

T34

T35	**£1**	Brown and green on white		
		Prefix coding: Letter and figure "1" over number ("dash").		
		Quantity printed: Included in T34 above.		
		Serial letters:		
		See below	75.00	45.00

Since the dash, or to be more accurate, the square dot, appears on random notes in particular sheets, it may be found under any serial letter. Most examples, however, have turned up with S1 serials.

For notes carrying the serial "Z" *see* under T16.

All Treasury notes of the third issue were replaced by Bank of England £1 and 10s. notes on 22 November 1928, but were still legal tender until the end of July 1933.

THE "CARLTON" POUND IN STAGES

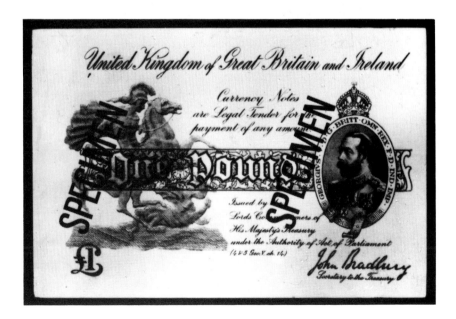

FISHER (contd.)

The "Carlton" Reverse

THE MACKENNAL POUND IN STAGES

The third stage is as T16 on page 14.

Mackennal's Reverse First type

Mackennal's Reverse Second type

A SELECTION OF REJECTED ESSAYS FROM THE BRADBURY THIRD ISSUE

Reverse of above note

FURTHER ESSAYS OF BRADBURY NOTES

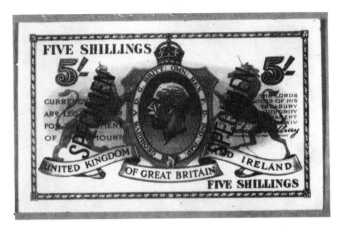

Bank of England Notes to 1928

The Bank of England was founded under a Royal Charter granted on 27 July 1964. During the reign of William and Mary (1689–1702) more money was needed to finance the War of the Grand Alliance against France. The idea for raising the money was put forward by a Scotsman, William Paterson, and a bill was drafted "for granting to their Majesties several rates and duties upon tunnage of ships and vessels and upon beer, ale and other liquors; for securing against certain recompenses and advantages in the said act mentioned, to such persons as shall voluntarily advance the sum of fifteen hundred thousand pounds towards carrying on the war against France." These recompenses and advantages were permission to set up "The Governor and Company of the Bank of England". The first governor was Sir John Houblon, his deputy was Mr. Michael Godfrey and there were 24 directors. Temporary offices were set up at the Mercers' Hall in Cheapside.

The first charter allowed the Bank to circulate notes up to the value of its capital of £1·2 million which was lent wholly to the government at 8% (yearly interest of £100,000). At this stage there was no guarantee of conversion of notes into gold, nor were the "running cash notes", as they were called, given the status of legal tender.

The three cashiers were appointed on 30 July 1694. The head cashier was John Kendrick (at a salary of £200 a year) and his assistants were Robert Hedges and Thomas Madockes. Mr. Kendrick's term was the shortest on record. He found the duties of the office "too onerous" and was allowed to step down on 11 August. Thomas Speed was appointed in his place, holding the post until 1699 and was then succeeded by Thomas Madockes (1699–1739). By the end of 1694 the Bank's business had been transferred from the Mercers' Hall to the nearby Grocers' Hall where it remained until the move to Threadneedle Street in June 1734.

Within two years, however, the fledgling bank was in trouble through no fault of its own. The problems arose from the passing of an Act in 1696 which ordered recoinage of the whole metallic currency. This had become hopelessly clipped and defaced, and naturally people, given the choice, wanted new and sound money, although the poor were largely unable to get it. Since the Bank's notes were not convertible they fell to a discount which at one stage was as high as 24%. Accounts submitted to Parliament on 4 December 1696 indicated that the £764,196 worth of notes outstanding were backed by only £35,664 of gold.

By March 1697 the position had been greatly eased, the problems of recoinage had been successfully overcome and on 1 April the Bank's charter was renewed until 1711 by Act of Parliament which provided that "no other bank or any corporation in the nature of a bank shall be established by Act of Parliament in this kingdom". A new subscription list was opened and the Bank's capital was increased by just over £1 million. The 1697 Act also contained a clause whereby the death penalty was to be imposed for forgery of the Bank's notes, though this was not to become a serious problem until the end of the 18th century.

In 1708 the Bank's monopoly was further strengthened by the veto of any notes payable on demand or at less than six months by joint stock banks with more than six partners. This was arguably the most important development in the early history of banking and was confirmed in the renewal of the Bank's charter in 1709 for 21 years and again when a 30 year renewal was enacted in 1713 following the Treaty of Utrecht.

The second major crisis for the Bank came in 1720 after the bursting of the South Sea Bubble. Bankruptcy was rife, people naturally wished to get hold of their money and the queue of those wishing to withdraw gold from the Bank stretched down Ludgate Hill to Fleet Street. The situation was saved by the ingenious expedient of employing its own staff to withdraw money in large quantities and then take it round to the back of the bank where it was redeposited! Thus were the tills kept open until public alarm subsided. A similar ploy was used with equal effect in 1745 when Bonnie Prince Charlie was marching on London.

The Bank's charter was renewed again in 1742, 1764 and 1781, the main development during these years being the rapid growth of small notes from the country banks (of six or fewer partners). Bank of England notes did not, of course, circulate much outside London. An attempt to stem the tide of paper was made in 1765 when it became illegal to issue notes for less than £1 other than on demand in Scotland, and the same was applied in England from 1775. Two years later this provision was extended when all notes of £1 and above and less than £5 had to carry the names and places of abode of persons to whose order they were made, and the signature attested by at least one witness. The effect was greatly to reduce the supply of £1 notes from the country banks (although this particular restriction did not apply to Scotland).

During this period the Bank enjoyed almost uninterrupted prosperity, but in February 1793 war was again declared between France and England and there followed a collapse of confidence. More than threequarters of the 400 country banks were forced to close in the next two or three years, despite the attempts by the Bank to alleviate the crisis. Napoleon was still relatively unknown but French activities were regularly reported and rumoured, and finally on 26 February 1797 the Bank itself stopped payment.

The *Bank Restriction Act* became law on 3 May 1797 under which the Bank was forbidden to pay cash for sums of twenty shillings or over to any creditor or use cash for any payment except to the Army or Navy, or Ordance on a Privy Council order. It was, however, stated that payment in the Bank's notes might be "legal tender by consent"—that is, if they were freely offered and accepted as such. The act was intended to be a temporary measure—in fact the bank did not resume full cash payments until 1 May 1821.

The famous £1 and £2 notes date from this time, bearing first the name of Abraham Newland (they were nicknamed "Newlands") and from 1807 that of Henry Hase. But confidence gradually returned and this was reflected in the fact that by 1810 the number of country banks had risen to more than 700. From November 1816 the Bank began to ease its restrictions which it was entitled to do on due notice, and notes under £5 issued before 1812 were exchangeable for cash. By September 1817, soon after the sovereign had become legal tender, the Bank was paying out on all notes issued prior to January 1817. Unfortunately the position again deteriorated and restrictions again had to be imposed until the end of January 1820.

Meanwhile legislation had been passed which put a fixed time on permission to issue notes below £5 to bearer on demand. This was to be two years after the resumption of cash payments (i.e. 1 May 1823). However, by an Act of 1822 this permission was extended to 1833 for all banks. It was not a wise decision and a massive expansion of credit followed. By 1825 country banks were collapsing right, left and centre, the most serious failure being that of Pole Thornton & Co. in September of that year. The consequences were so severe that the Bank had to use all its resources to stem the panic—even to the extent of using an old stock of 600,000 £1 notes from the restriction period. In December 1825 the Bank's own resources fell as low as £1¼ million compared to £13½ million in 1824.

It was these events which brought the series of Acts over the next 18 years on which the modern banking system is based. The first of these in 1826 underlined the belief in the need for reliable joint stock banks. The Bank's monopoly was restricted to within 65 miles of London, thus making it possible for the first time for joint stock banks with more than six partners to operate outside the limit. These banks were able to issue their own notes of £5 and above. Existing notes of less than £5 payable to bearer on demand were to be redeemed not later than 5 April 1829. At the same time the Bank was allowed to open branches anywhere in England—the first such branch was at Gloucester on 19 July 1826.

In the 1833 *Bank Charter Act*, Bank of England notes were made legal tender for the first time on all sums above £5 except at the Bank itself so long as they were convertible to legal coin (this apparently strange proviso was to enable individual £5 notes to be changed into gold for the payment of wages). The act also permitted the establishment of joint stock banks within 65 miles of the capital provided that they were for deposit only and did not issue their own notes. The first such bank, the London and Westminster, opened its doors in London, in March 1834.

The 1830s were times of boom and speculation, especially in railways, and once again credit was created on a massive scale leading to the inevitable collapses. The country note issue expanded by 50% in 1836 alone. It was against this background that Sir Robert Peel introduced the most far-reaching Act of all. The *Bank Charter Act* of 1844 (passed on 19 July), finally put a stop to the free-for-all and put strict controls on note issuing. By this stage there were more than 200 private banks and 72 joint stock banks still going strong. Under the Act new banks were forbidden to issue notes, limits were set on existing banks and if a bank was wound up or amalgamated, the right of issue was forfeited and the Bank of England took over two thirds of the lapsed amount. Just over 75 years later the final country note issue ceased when Fox Fowler & Co. of Wellington, Somerset merged with Lloyds Bank in October 1921.

Despite the railway crisis of 1847, the American crisis of 1857, the crash of the Overend Gurney Bank in 1866 and the Baring crisis of 1890, the pre-eminence of the Bank of England was never seriously challenged after the *Bank Charter Act* of 1844. As Richard B. Kimball wrote in *Popular Monthly* in 1882: "The credit of England and the credit of the Bank of England are convertible terms".

The Earliest Medallion—1697. Note signed by Thomas Madockes.

Bank Note of 1699.

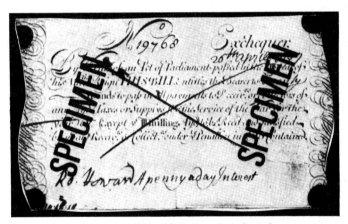

Exchequer Bill with both ends indented

Early Issues

Running Cash Notes

Running cash notes derive from the goldsmith notes which had been widely used by merchants from the reign of Charles I. The running cash note was a receipt for a deposit made out to bearer so that he could use it in a business transaction or present it to the Bank for gold or silver. The first two chief cashiers were:

John Kendrick (1694) and Thomas Speed (1694–99)

The notes were entirely written by hand and, at first, were written on ordinary paper purchased from a stationers—a practice which soon ceased because of forgery. These notes could be part-paid. The holder could draw £5 from a note issued for £10 and have it duly recorded on the note, retaining the note as his receipt for the remaining £5 deposited in the Bank of England.

At first running cash notes were issued for odd amounts but before long they were made out for regular amounts. No examples are known to be in private hands.

Sealed Bills

These were not banknotes in the strict sense as they were promissory notes, normally bearing interest, issued against deposits or pledged assets. If they were intended to circulate from hand to hand they were unsuccessful and within twenty years went out of use altogether.

Accomptable Notes

Introduced four days after the running cash notes, these were certificates of deposit and were not intended to serve as banknotes. They gave the depositor the right to "draw notes" on the Bank of England. Such withdrawals were then endorsed on the accomptable note. At a later date special forms were prepared by the Bank of England with a "check" pattern. The drawn notes were written by depositors on these forms which thus became an early version of the modern cheque.

It is interesting to note that the sealed bills, running cash notes and accomptable notes were all introduced in the first week of the Bank of England's existence. The first meeting of the Court of Directors of the Bank of England on 27 July 1694 was concerned with the ". . . method of giving Receipts for running cash. . .". The first decision was that "running cash notes" should be issued.

In *The Bank of England Note*, Mackenzie reports that in 1695 there was a short-lived issue of printed denominations of £5, £10, £20, £30, £40, £50 and £100. The notes were numbered A to G, the order was placed on 5 June 1695 and the printing was carried out by the Bank's stationer, William Staresmore. None has survived.

Part-printed Notes

The first partially printed notes of the Bank have a medallion of Britannia seated and holding a spear and olive branch, possibly the work of John Sturt. For the most part these notes only circulated within a 20 mile radius of London and the earliest known notes are those signed by:

Thomas Madockes (1699–1739)

Notes continued to be issued for handwritten amounts, but in 1707 the design was the Britannia medallion modified to show a foliate border surround, and from 1725, 14 denominations were printed by copper plate:

1725–82

Henry Portal paper. Printed by copper-plate. Black on white. Denominations: £20, £30, £40, £50, £60, £70, £80, £90, £100, £200, £300, £400, £500, £1000. (dates of first issue vary).

James Collier and Daniel Race (1739–51)

Notes continued to be issued in the 14 denominations above. By 1745 notes were all printed in "round" figures. However, the word "pounds" was not printed so that an odd amount could still be written by hand if required. The Bank has one note for £28 10s on which the words "eight pounds ten shillings" have been written after the printed "twenty".

Daniel Race and Elias Simes (1751–59)

From 1752 the handwritten name of the payee was usually that of the Chief Cashier. In 1759 two further denominations for £10 and £15 were issued and for the first time the word "pound" or "pounds" was printed after the amount. Other denominations continued to have "pounds" handwritten until the end of the century.

Daniel Race (1759–75)

Notes continued to be issued for the 16 denominations above and in 1765 a note for £25 was added with the word "pounds" printed on it.

Charles Jewson (1775–77)

There were no developments of significance during Mr. Jewson's term of office.

Note: At the time of writing no banknote prior to the Newland period is known to be in private hands. It has therefore been decided not to start formal numbering before Newland, and thereafter each Chief Cashier is allocated a "master" number only covering all the appropriate notes. In most cases collectors may well count themselves fortunate to obtain a single example of each Chief Cashier.

Abraham Newland (1778–1807)

The son of a miller and baker of Southwark, Newland entered service in 1748 and succeeded Charles Jewson as Chief Cashier on 8 January 1778 and held office until September 1807. His name became a household word during the restriction period from 1797 and £1 notes were often referred to as "Newlands". History relates that his commitment to business was such that he never slept away from the Bank. A confirmed batchelor, he amassed a fortune of £200,000, declined a pension and was instead given a piece of silverplate to the value of 1000 guineas.

From 1752 until 1781 the handwritten name of the payee was usually, but not invariably, that of the Chief Cashier. In fact the oldest note so far recorded in private hands, £50 dated 13 April 1780, is not payable to Newland. From 1782 the Chief Cashier's name was used exclusively until 1885 when notes were made payable simply "to bearer".

1778

Printed by copper plate on paper produced by Henry Portal. Black on white. £10, £15, £20, £25, £30, £40, £50, £60, £70, £80, £90, £100, £200, £300, £400, £500, £1000.

The £60, £70, £80, £90 and £400 were no longer issued after 1803.

In 1793, the economic difficulties caused by the Napoleonic War with France made small denominations necessary, starting with a £5 note. This was followed in 1797 by the £1 and £2 notes, issued on 2 March. It seems that there are four different types of £1 and five different types of £2 note. Printed by copper plate on paper produced by Henry Portal.

Price

B200	£1	Black on white (1797) (handwritten number, date, cashier and signatures)
	£1	Black on white (1798–1801) (smaller plate, printed cashier's name)
	£1	Black on white (1801–1803) (standard large size)
	£1	Black on white (1803–1807) (as above with value in watermark)
	£2	Black on white (1797–1805) (four varieties as above £1)
	£2	Black on white (1805–1807 (new design)
	£5	Black on white

Newland £1 notes

Newland £1 notes

Newland £2 and £5 notes

Henry Hase (1807–29)

The "reluctant" Chief Cashier. Hase came to office only because of the fall of the second cashier, Robert Aslett who was found guilty of embezzling half a million pounds in 1803. Aslett had taken Exchequer Bills amounting to £200,000 and had lodged these as security for advances with a lottery office keeper in Cornhill. He escaped the death penalty and was imprisoned in Newgate until 1820 when he was pardoned on condition he left the country. Hase was not dedicated to the Bank in the way that Newland had been and he died in 1829 at a comparatively young age.

1807

Printed by copper plate on paper produced by Henry Portal. From 1807 the name of the Chief Cashier is printed as payee. From 1808 the dates and serial numbers are printed, so the only part of the note not printed is the signature(s). This remained the case until 1853.

			Price VF
B201	£1	Black on white (handwritten date, countersigned)	from £500
	£1	Black on white (handwritten date, not countersigned)	
	£1	Black on white (printed date and serial numbers)	
	£1	Black on white (1825–26 emergency issue) (top date 1821)	

The emergency issue can be identified by the date at the top reading 1821 but the date of issue is four or five years later.

	£2	Black on white (handwritten date, countersigned)
	£2	Black on white (handwritten date, not countersigned)
	£2	Black on white (printed date and serial numbers)
	£5	Black on white (handwritten)
	£5	Black on white (printed date and serial numbers)

Hase notes were also issued in the following 12 denominations:
£10, £15, £20, £25, £30, £40, £50, £100, £200, £300, £500, £1000

None are known to have survived in private hands at the time of writing. The £15 and £25 notes were withdrawn from 1822. Branch notes were first issued during the Hase period.

Hase notes, B201

Hase notes, B201

BRANCH NOTES

Following the Bank Act of 1826, when joint stock banks were permitted to operate outside the 65 mile radius of London, the Bank was able to open branches and branch notes date from this period. Virtually none has survived from the 19th century and it is thus impossible to price the notes.

Henry Hase branch notes were issued from:

1. Gloucester (opened 19 July 1826)
2. Manchester (opened 21 September 1826)
3. Swansea (opened 23 October 1826)
4. Birmingham (opened 1 January 1827)
5. Liverpool (opened 2 July 1827)
6. Bristol (opened 12 July 1827)
7. Leeds (opened 23 August 1827)
8. Exeter (opened 17 December 1827)
9. Newcastle (opened 21 April 1828)

House at Exeter once occupied as a branch of the
Bank of England.

The Portsmouth branch of the Bank of England in 1913.

Thomas Rippon (1829–35)

The son of a baptist minister of Up Ottery, Devon, he entered service with the Bank in 1782. With the dismissal of Robert Aslett in 1803, Rippon was promoted from third clerk in the drawing office to second cashier. When Henry Hase became Chief Cashier in 1807, Rippon was appointed as his chief assistant. He became Chief Cashier himself at the age of 70 in 1829 and remained in office until his death on 10 August 1835. Rippon declared himself nowhere so happy as in his business and supposedly took only one holiday during his entire career with the Bank.

1829

Printed by copper plate on paper produced by Henry Portal.

			Price
B202	**£5**	Black on white	–
	£10	Black on white	–

Rippon notes were also issued in the following nine denominations: £20, £30, £40, £50, £100, £200, £300, £500, £1000.

Rippon branch notes were issued from: Birmingham, Bristol, Exeter (closed 30 April 1834), Gloucester, Hull (opened 2 January 1829), Leeds, Liverpool, Manchester, Newcastle, Norwich (opened 19 November 1829), Plymouth (opened 1 May 1834), Portsmouth (opened 16 May 1834) and Swansea.

B202

Matthew Marshall (1835–64)

No biographical information is available on the career of Matthew Marshall, who presided over the major commercial crisis of 1857 during which two banks in Liverpool failed. By November of that year the Bank of England was virtually the only bank prepared to discount bills of exchange.

There were three different series of Marshall notes. The first series from 1835–53 is the same as those of Thomas Rippon with various handwritten signatures. From 1853–55 notes were printed bearing signatures: J. Vautin, H. Bock, J. Ferraby, J. Williams, J. Luson. From 1855, the third series replaced the name of the Chief Cashier with the words: "I promise to pay the Bearer on Demand". At the same time Matthew Marshall's signature was introduced into the watermark and the vignette of Britannia was redesigned by Daniel Maclise R.A. In 1860 new signatures were introduced: W. P. Gattie, T. Kent and C. T. Whitmel (all printed as before).

1835

Plate printed on paper manufactured by Henry Portal.

			Price VF
B203	**£5**	Black on white (handwritten signature)	from £1000
	£5	Black on white (printed signature)	
	£5	Black on white (payable to bearer)	
	£10	Black on white (handwritten signature)	
	£10	Black on white (printed signature)	
	£10	Black on white (payable to bearer)	

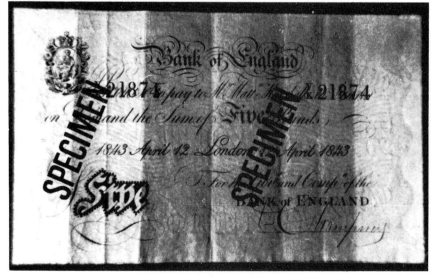

B203

Marshall notes were also issued in the following nine denominations:
£20, £30, £40, £50, £100, £200, £300, £500, £1000 (*see* frontispiece).

The £40 note was withdrawn in 1851 and the £30 in 1852.
Marshall branch notes were issued from Birmingham, Bristol, Gloucester
(closed 28 February 1849), Hull, Leeds, Leicester (opened 1 January
1844), Liverpool, Manchester, Newcastle, Norwich (closed 31 March
1852), Plymouth, Portsmouth and Swansea (closed 28 February 1859).

The Bank Medallion. From the original Pencil Design by Daniel
Maclise, R.A.

William Miller (1864–66)

The short term of office of Mr. Miller seems to be largely undocumented. There appears to be no such thing as a "Miller" note; when Marshall's signature was removed from the watermark, for unknown reasons Miller's signature was not substituted. Printed signatures were: W. P. Gattie, T. Kent and C. T. Whitmel.

1864

Plate printed on paper manufactured by Henry Portal.

			Price
B204	**£5**	Black on White	–
	£10	Black on white	–

Miller notes were also issued in the following seven denominations:
£20, £50, £100, £200, £300, £500, £1000.

Miller branch notes were issued from Birmingham, Bristol, Hull, Leeds, Leicester, Liverpool, Manchester, Newcastle, Plymouth and Portsmouth.

George Forbes (1866–73)

No biographical information is available on the career of Mr. Forbes.
There are two types of Forbes notes. The first contains Mr. Forbes' signature in the watermark and carries the printed signatures of other bank staff: H. Dixon, T. Puzey or W. O. Wheeler. From 1 November 1870 the printed signature of the Chief Cashier appears on all Bank of England notes together with the words "Chief Cashier" under his name.

1866

Plate printed on paper manufactured by Henry Portal. Notes printed two to a sheet and cut to give one straight edge and three deckle edges.

			Price
B205	**£5**	Black on white (signed H. Dixon)	–
	£5	Black on white (signed G. Forbes from 1870)	–
	£10	Black on white (signed H. Dixon)	–
	£10	Black on white (signed G. Forbes from 1870)	–

Forbes notes were also issued in the following seven denominations:
£20, £50, £100, £200, £300, £500, £1000.

Forbes branch notes were issued from Birmingham, Bristol, Hull, Leeds, Leicester (closed 29 February 1872), Liverpool, Manchester, Newcastle, Plymouth and Portsmouth.

Forbes £5 note signed by H. Dixon.

STANLEY GIBBONS SAFE 'N' CLEAR DISPLAY SYSTEM

Stanley Gibbons *Safe 'n' Clear* leaves are ideal for displaying bank notes. The entire system is manufactured only from the highest quality materials guaranteed to give maximum protection. The leaves are of tough matt-black board, colour-fast and completely free of potentially harmful chemicals. The crystal-clear polyester strips contain no softners, acids, solvents or plasticisers and offer substantial protection against ultra-violet radiation, humidity and friction. The bonding between strips and leaf is similarly chemically inert, ensuring that leaves will not warp or buckle under adverse conditions, whilst holding bank notes firmly in place. Leaves are multipunched to fit a vast range of binders from 2 to 22 ring, whatever ring sytem you are using at present, *Safe 'n' Clear* will probably fit it.

There is also a *Safe 'n' Clear Binder* – with a luxuriously padded cover in royal blue and a subtle gold blocked border on the front and spine. It has a four 'D' ring mechanism for easy turning and neat stacking of leaves.

Safe 'n' Clear leaves and binders are available from the Stanley Gibbons shop at 399 Strand, London WC2 or by post from: Stanley Gibbons Publications Ltd, 5 Parkside, Christchurch Rd., Ringwood, Hants, BH24 3SH. Send for our brochure and price list.

Orders may be placed by phone quoting your credit card number – Ringwood (042 54) 2363

Frank May (1873–93)

Following in the steps of his father, May entered service with the Bank in 1852 and rose to Chief Cashier on 30 July 1873. However, in 1893 he was dismissed having "totally misconceived the nature of his trust" by favouring certain customers, mostly in the Stock Exchange, without the permission of the governor. May had allowed unauthorised overdrafts and had waived interest payments on other accounts. May ended his days in obscurity in his home town of Bath. The committee of enquiry which investigated the whole affair concluded that the Chief Cashier should become the highest paid official of the Bank thereafter.

1873

Plate printed on paper manufactured by Henry Portal. Notes printed two to a sheet and cut to give one straight edge and three deckle edges.

		Price VF
B206 **£5**	Black on white	£1300
£10	Black on white	£1625

May notes were also issued in the following seven denominations: £20, £50, £100, £200, £300, £500, £1000.

The £300 note was withdrawn in 1885.

May branch notes were issued from: Birmingham, Bristol, Hull, Leeds, Liverpool, Manchester, Newcastle, Plymouth and Portsmouth.

B206

B206 (Bristol Branch)

Horace George Bowen (1893–1902)

Bowen served as Chief Accountant from 1888 and succeeded Frank May on 9 November 1893. The immediate consequence of May's disgrace was the setting up of a committee to report on "Officers' emoluments and safeguards for due control of advances and overdrafts and accounts generally, and the manner in which the services of the committee in daily waiting may be best employed".

1893

Plate printed on paper manufactured by Henry Portal. Notes printed two to a sheet and cut to give one straight edge and three deckle edges.

			Price VF
B207	**£5**	Black on white	£1250
	£10	Black on white	£1600

Bowen notes were also issued in the following six denominations:
£20, £50, £100, £200, £500, £1000.

Bowen branch notes were issued from: Birmingham, Bristol, Hull, Leeds, Liverpool, Manchester, Newcastle, Plymouth and Portsmouth.

B207

John Gordon Nairne (1902–18)

Entered Bank service in 1880. Chief Cashier 1902. Comptroller 1918. Director 1925–31.

1902

Plate printed on paper manufactured by Henry Portal. Notes printed two to a sheet and cut to give one straight edge and three deckle edges.

			Price VF
B208	**£5**	Black on white	£225
	£10	Black on white	£325
	£20	Black on white	£500
	£50	Black on white	£875

Nairne notes were also issued in the following four denominations: £100, £200, £500, £1000.

Nairne branch notes were issued from: Birmingham, Bristol, Hull, Leeds, Liverpool, Manchester, Newcastle, Plymouth and Portsmouth (closed 30 April 1914).

Note: Nairne notes issued prior to 1914 are considerably scarcer than those issued during the First World War.

B208

B208

During the summer of 1914 it became increasingly clear to both the Treasury and Bank of England officials that some form of paper money of a lower denomination than £5 would have to be substituted for the gold sovereign. The question was who would issue it. The Bank had no doubts about its claim and made preparations. The Bank £1 note in its proof form, shown above, ranks as one of the major varieties of the English series. Only four copies are known.

Ernest Musgrave Harvey (1918–25)

Entered Bank service in 1885. Deputy Chief Cashier 1902. Chief Cashier 1918. Comptroller 1925. Director 1928–29. Deputy Governor 1929–36. Awarded C.B.E. 1917. K.B.E. 1920. Baronet 1933. Chevalier of the Legion of Honour 1918. Chevalier of the Order of Leopold of Belguim 1919.

1918

Plate printed on paper manufactured by Henry Portal. Notes printed two to a sheet and cut to give one straight edge and three deckle edges.

			Price VF
B209	**£5**	Black on white	£85
	£10	Black on white	£185
	£20	Black on white	£450
	£50	Black on white	£550
	£100	Black on white	£650
	£200	Black on white	–
	£500	Black on white	–
	£1000	Black on white	–

For full prefix details see page 172.

Note: Harvey notes issued prior to 1920 are considerably scarcer than those issued subsequently.

B209

B209

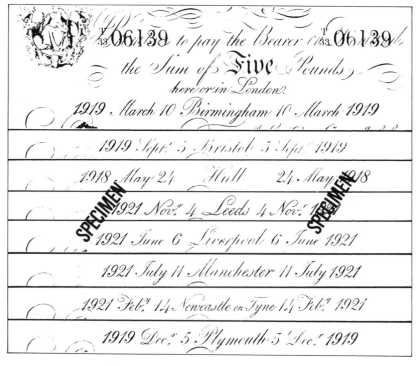

Date lines for each of the branch banks

Ernest Harvey and all subsequent branch notes were
issued, in ascending order of rarity, from:

1. Leeds	5. Newcastle on Tyne
2. Manchester	6. Hull
3. Liverpool	7. Bristol
4. Birmingham	8. Plymouth

St. Luke's Printing Works (Bank of England), Old Street, E.C.1.

Modern Bank of England Notes (from 1928)

The Bank of England assumed the responsibility of the printing and issue of currency notes on 28 November 1928, under the *Currency and Banknotes Act* 1928, and in July 1933 the Treasury notes were withdrawn from circulation.

The Bank's first issue (Series A) of green £1 notes and red-brown 10s. notes, referred to by collectors as "Britannia" notes, were signed by the Chief Cashier, C. P. Mahon, and joined the existing high-denomination notes of £5 and above.

In June 1931, after consulting the Royal Mint Advisory Committee, the Bank invited three artists to compete with a view to future note designs, Stephen Gooden, Frederick Landseer Griggs and Kruger Gray. As a result Gooden was appointed as the Bank's designer, but the various essays that he produced during the 1930s were not taken up.

In 1940, following the outbreak of war, the colour of the £1 and 10s. notes was changed to blue and mauve respectively and a metal thread—the invention of Mr. S. B. Chamberlain, General Manager of the Bank's Printing Works—was inserted.

In 1943, following the appearance of German forgeries, it was decided to withdraw the denominations above £5. It was 20 years before the £10 was to reappear, nearly 30 years before the country again had a £20 note and nearly 40 years to the return of a £50 note.

One problem that the Bank faced during the War was the difficulty in transporting coinage. In view of this small-denomination notes of 2s. 6d. and 5s. were prepared, but they were not needed. The notes were supposedly all destroyed after the War, but a few specimens survived and have found their way into the hands of collectors.

In 1948 £1 and 10s. notes of the pre-war colours, green and red-brown, were again issued and for a short time were unthreaded to use up old stocks of paper. Subsequently all Bank of England notes incorporated the now familiar metal thread as a security precaution.

During the early 1950s Stephen Gooden prepared a new series of notes depicting the first Governor of the Bank, Sir John Houblon. They were not issued. He followed this with a series featuring a Lion and Key and the helmeted head of Britannia, from which the £5 (Series B) was issued in 1957 to replace the traditional white fiver.

Meanwhile, in July 1956, it was announced that H.M. The Queen had agreed to her portrait being included on a new series of notes. Stephen Gooden had died on 21 September 1955 and the designs for this issue (Series C), known to collectors as the "Portrait" series were undertaken by Robert Austin.

On 19 November 1959 the Bank formally announced that the new notes would appear early in 1960 and on 17 March the £1 appeared, followed some 18 months later by the 10s.; then in 1963 came the £5 and in 1964 the £10. These last two were the work of Reynolds Stone who was retained by the Bank from 1959, and on the £5 note he used his daughter as the model for the "child Britannia" on the reverse.

In 1970 the first in a new and more imaginative series of designs appeared (Series D), known to collectors as the "Pictorial" series. Designed by Harry Eccleston, who had joined the Bank in 1958, the reverse of each note carries an historical scene: The £1 (1978) has Sir Isaac Newton with his telescope seated under an apple tree; the £5 (1971) features the Duke of Wellington and a battle scene from the Peninsular War; the £10 (1975) depicts Florence Nightingale and a hospital scene from the Crimean War; the £20 (1970) shows a statue of William Shakespeare with the balcony scene from *Romeo and Juliet*; and the £50 (1981) incorporates Sir Christopher Wren and a view of St. Paul's Cathedral from the River Thames.

On 27 January 1981, it was announced by the Chancellor, Sir Geoffrey Howe, in the House of Commons that a £1 coin would be issued in 1983. At the time of writing it remains to be seen when (or whether) the £1 note will be phased out.

A rejected essay of the 1920s

Proofs of designs for the £1 vignette surrounds

The model for the watermark of Britannia's head

SERIES A ("BRITANNIA") 1928–1962

On 22 November 1928 the Bank of England £1 note was reintroduced after a gap of more than 100 years and the 10s. note was introduced for the first time. The new banknotes were signed by the Chief Cashier, C. P. Mahon, and replaced the various Treasury notes issued since 1914. The designs, approved in 1927, were a collective effort by the architect, W. M. Keesey (responsible for the reverse of both notes) and other experts inside and outside the Bank. The obverse of the notes showed the medallion of Britannia seated by Daniel Maclise (originally used for the high-denomination notes from 1855). Keesey's reverse of the £1 showed the south front of the Bank prior to rebuilding and vignettes of St. George and the Dragon used by Benedetto Pistrucci in his design for the sovereign. These were contained within swirls of acanthus leaves in a blend of pale green, blue and mauve. A similar background in red-brown was used for the reverse of the 10s. surrounding the two value tablets. The notes were plate-printed in sheets of 24 at St. Luke's Works, Old Street, London, on banknote paper manufactured by Portals Ltd, with a watermark of wavy lines and the helmeted head of Britannia facing right. "Britannia" £1 notes—as they are termed by collectors—measure 151 × 85 mm (6 × 3⅜ in.) and were legal tender until 28 may 1962. The 10s. notes measure 140 × 78 mm (5½ × 3¹/₁₆ in.) and were legal tender until 29 October 1962.

The listings are arranged below under the name of each Chief Cashier, beginning with C. P. Mahon.

STANLEY GIBBONS SAFE 'N' CLEAR DISPLAY SYSTEM

Stanley Gibbons *Safe 'n' Clear* leaves are ideal for displaying bank notes. The entire system is manufactured only from the highest quality materials guaranteed to give maximum protection. The leaves are of tough matt-black board, colour-fast and completely free of potentially harmful chemicals. The crystal-clear polyester strips contain no softners, acids, solvents or plasticisers and offer substantial protection against ultra-violet radiation, humidity and friction. The bonding between strips and leaf is similarly chemically inert, ensuring that leaves will not warp or buckle under adverse conditions, whilst holding bank notes firmly in place. Leaves are multipunched to fit a vast range of binders from 2 to 22 ring, whatever ring sytem you are using at present, *Safe 'n' Clear* will probably fit it.

There is also a *Safe 'n' Clear Binder* – with a luxuriously padded cover in royal blue and a subtle gold blocked border on the front and spine. It has a four 'D' ring mechanism for easy turning and neat stacking of leaves.

Safe 'n' Clear leaves and binders are available from the Stanley Gibbons shop at 399 Strand, London WC2 or by post from: Stanley Gibbons Publications Ltd, 5 Parkside, Christchurch Rd., Ringwood, Hants, BH24 3SH. Send for our brochure and price list.

Orders may be placed by phone quoting your credit card number – Ringwood (042 54) 2363

Cyril Patrick Mahon (1925–29)

Born 1882. Entered Bank service 1901. Chief Cashier 1 April 1925 to 26 March 1929. Comptroller 1929–32.

		Price	
		EF	*VF*

B210 **10s.** Red-brown
　　　　Prefix coding: Letter, number, number.
　　　　Width of design: 126 mm.
　　　　Quantity printed: 410 million.
　　　　Serial letters:

		EF	*VF*
A01 (one million notes of inaugural run)		£250	£175
Z—(first series traced from Z01)		60·00	35·00
Y—, X—, W—	*each*	50·00	30·00
V—(last series traced to V11)		£165	95·00

B210

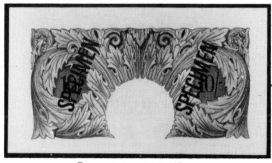

Common reverse to 10s.

MAHON (contd.)

B212

Common reverse to Britannia £1 from Mahon to O'Brien

<table>
<tr><td></td><td colspan="2">Price</td></tr>
<tr><td></td><td>EF</td><td>VF</td></tr>
</table>

B211 **10s.** Red-brown replacement note
 Prefix coding: Not known.
 Quantity printed: Not known.
 Serial letters: Not yet traced.

B212 **£1** Green
 Prefix coding: Letter, number, number.
 Width of design (i.e. signature block):
  Plate 1: 137·5 mm.
  Plate 2: 138·5 mm.
 Quantity printed: 725 million.
 Serial letters:

		Price EF	VF
A01 (one million notes of inaugural run).		£250	£175
A—(first series traced from A02)		60·00	35·00
B—, C—, D—, E—, F—, G—	*each*	45·00	25·00
H—(last series traced to H32)		60·00	35·00

No price distinction between plates 1 and 2 notes.

B214 £1

B214 10s. with matching serial number

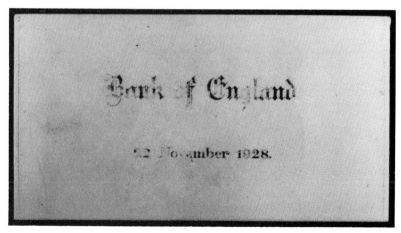

B214 envelope

MAHON (contd.)

B213 **£1**   Green replacement note   *   *
Prefix coding: Not known.
Quantity printed: Not known.
Serial letters: Not yet traced.

B214   £1 and 10s. notes with matching serial
numbers in presentation parchment
envelope, inscribed "BANK OF ENGLAND
22 November 1928". 100 pairs only beli-
eved issued.   Price *(EF)* from £1250

For classification of specimen notes and errors *see* page 149.

1925 (date unknown)

Large denomination notes from FIVE POUNDS TO ONE THOUSAND POUNDS,
bearing various dates between 1925 and 1929, were issued with the signature of C. P. Mahon. Of traditional design, lettering and watermark, these
notes measured 212 × 135 mm (8⅜ × 5⁵/₁₆ in.) and were plate-printed in
pairs (the cut leaving one straight edge and three deckled) at St. Luke's
Works, London, on banknote paper manufactured by Portals Ltd. Notes of
£10 and above were legal tender until 1 May 1945, and £5 notes without
metal thread until 1 March 1946.
For full prefix details *see* page 172.

B215

			Price	
			EF	*VF*
B215 **£5**	Black on white (from 18 April 1925)		£145	80·00
B216 **£10**	Black on white		£185	£100
B217 **£20**	Black on white		£450	£250
B218 **£50**	Black on white		£550	£350
B219 **£100**	Black on white		£850	£485
B220 **£200**	Black on white (discontinued 1928)		–	–
B221 **£500**	Black on white		from £4000	
B222 **£1000**	Black on white		from £7500	

Branch notes as Ernest Harvey (*see* page 69).

Basil Gage Catterns (1929–34)

Born 1886. Entered Bank service 1908, Chief Cashier 27 March 1929 to 17 April 1934. Director 1934–36 and 1945–48, Deputy Governor 1936–45.

B223

1930 (15 July) TEN SHILLINGS

Design, watermark and dimensions as for C. P. Mahon, but larger plates used for some notes. Printed at St. Luke's Works, London.

	Price	
	EF	*VF*

B223 **10s.** Red-brown
    Prefix coding: Letter, number, number.
    Width of design:
      Plate 1: 126 mm.
      Plate 2: 128 mm.
    Quantity printed: 965 million.
    Serial letters:

		EF	*VF*
V—(first series traced from V14)		40·00	25·00
U—, T—, S—, R—, O—, N—, M—,			
L—	*each*	32·00	20·00
K—(last series traced to K99)		38·00	24·00

For plate 2 notes add 20% to the above prices.

B224	Red-brown replacement note	*	*

    Prefix coding: Not known.
    Quantity printed: Not known.
    Serial letters: Not yet traced.

1930 (15 July) ONE POUND

Design, watermark and dimensions as for C. P. Mahon, but larger plates used for some notes. Printed at St. Luke's Works, London.

<table>
<tr><td></td><td></td><td></td><td colspan="2">*Price*</td></tr>
<tr><td></td><td></td><td></td><td>*EF*</td><td>*VF*</td></tr>
</table>

B225 £1   Green

Prefix coding: Letter, number, number.

Width of design (i.e. signature block):

    Plate 1: 137·5 mm.

    Plate 2: 138·5 mm.

Quantity printed: 1450 million

Serial letters:

H—(first series traced from H33)		40·00	25·00
J—, K—, L—, M—, N—, O—, R—,			
S—, T—, U—, W—, X—, Y— *each*		25·00	14·00
Z—(last series traced to Z99)		35·00	20·00

No price distinction between plate 1 and plate 2 notes.

B226 £1   Green

Prefix coding: Number, number, letter

Width of design (i.e., signature block):

    138·5 mm.

Quantity printed: 99 million.

Serial letters:

—A (series traced from 01A to 99A)	75·00	55·00

B227 £1   Green replacement note   *   *

Prefix coding: Not known.

Quantity printed: Not known.

Serial letters: Not yet traced.

For classification of specimen notes and errors *see* page 149.

B225

CATTERNS (contd.)

B229

B232 Bristol Branch note

1929 (date unknown)

Large denomination notes from FIVE POUNDS to ONE THOUSAND POUNDS, bearing various dates between 1929 and 1934. Design, watermark and dimensions as for C. P. Mahon notes. Printed at St. Luke's Works, London. For prefix details *see* page 172.

			Price	
			EF	*VF*
B228 **£5**	Black on white (from 27 March 1929)		£145	80·00
B229 **£10**	Black on white		£185	£100
B230 **£20**	Black on white		£450	£250
B231 **£50**	Black on white		£550	£350
B232 **£100**	Black on white		£850	£485
B233 **£500**	Black on white		from £4000	
B234 **£1000**	Black on white		from £7000	

Branch notes as Ernest Harvey (*see* page 69).

Kenneth Oswald Peppiatt (1934–49)

Born 1893. Entered Bank service 1911. Chief Cashier 18 April 1934 to 28 February 1949. Director 1949–57, K.B.E. 1941.

FIRST PERIOD (1934–39)

1934 (5 October) TEN SHILLINGS

Design, watermark and dimensions as for C. P. Mahon, but larger plates used for some notes. Printed at St. Luke's Works, London.

		Price	
		EF	*VF*
B235 10s.	Red-brown		
	Prefix coding: Letter, number, number.		
	Width of design:		
	Plate 1: 126 mm.		
	Plate 2: 128 mm.		
	Quantity printed: 693 million.		
	Serial letters:		
	J—(first series traced from J01)	45·00	25·00
	H—, E—, D—, C—, B— *each*	40·00	22·00
	A—(last series traced to A99)	45·00	25·00

For plate 2 notes add 25% to the above prices.

B236 10s.	Red-brown		
	Prefix coding: Number, number, letter.		
	Width of design:		
	Plate 1: 126 mm.		
	Plate 2: 128 mm.		
	Quantity printed: 850 million.		
	Serial letters:		
	—Z (first series traced from 01Z)	45.00	25·00
	—Y, —X, —W, —U, —T, —S, —R *each*	38·00	23·00
	—O (last series traced to 79O)	45·00	25·00

No examples have been found of serial letters —N and —M which were probably destroyed in the blitz in 1940. For plate 2 notes add 10% to the above prices.

B237 10s.	Red-brown replacement note	*	*
	Prefix coding: Not known.		
	Quantity printed: Not known.		
	Serial letters: Not yet traced.		

B235

B236 .

1934 (17 October) ONE POUND

Design, watermark and dimensions as for C. P. Mahon notes. Printed at St. Luke's Works, London.

			Price	
			EF	*VF*
B238 £1	Green			
	Prefix coding: Number, number, letter.			
	Width of design-signature block: 138·5 mm.			
	Quantity printed: 1880 million.			
	Serial letters:			
	—B (first series traced from 01B)		38·00	23·00
	—C, —D, —E, —H, —J, —K, —L, —M, —N, —O, —R, —S, —T, —U, —W, —X, —Y	*each*	25·00	16·00
	—Z (last series traced to 99Z)		35·00	19·00

PEPPIATT (contd.)

B238

			Price	
			EF	*VF*

B239 **£1**   Green
    Prefix coding: Letter, number, number,
       letter.
    Width of design (i.e. signature block):
       138·5 mm.
    Quantity printed: 850 million.
    Serial letters:

A—A (first series traced from A03A)		28·00	18·00
B—A, C—A, D—A, E—A, H—A,			
J—A, K—A	*each*	25·00	16·00
L—A (last series traced to L39A)		35·00	19·00

No examples have been found of serial letters M—A, N—A and O—A,
which were probably destroyed in the blitz of 1940.

B239

			Price	
			EF	VF
B240 £1	Green replacement note		*	*

Prefix coding: Not known.
Quantity printed: Not known.
Serial letters: Not yet traced.

For classification of specimen notes and errors *see* page 149.

1934 (August)

Large denomination notes from FIVE POUNDS to ONE THOUSAND POUNDS, bearing various dates between August 1934 and August 1943. Design, watermark and dimensions as for C. P. Mahon notes. Printed at St. Luke's Works, London.
For prefix details *see* page 173.

B241 £5	Black on white (from 1 May 1934)	65·00	45·00
B242 £10	Black on white	£135	85·00
B243 £20	Black on white	£350	£285
B244 £50	Black on white	£450	£250
B245 £100	Black on white	£650	£425
B246 £500	Black on white	from £2500	
B247 £1000	Black on white	from £6500	

Branch notes of Ernest Harvey (*see* page 69).
The office at Hull closed on 28 February 1939. All branch notes were discontinued at the outbreak of war in 1939.

B243

PEPPIATT (contd.)

SECOND PERIOD (1940–48)

1940 (29 March) ONE POUND

The blue emergency issue incorporating a metal thread—the invention of the General Manager of the Bank's printing works, Mr. S. B. Chamberlain. Basic design and dimensions unchanged, but a double line surrounded the unprinted part of the front containing the Britannia watermark. Plate-printed ("A" series only) until September 1940 at St. Luke's Works, London, on banknote paper manufactured by Portals Ltd. Thereafter by offset-litho at Overton, Hampshire. Emergency issue £1 notes were legal tender until 28 May 1962.

		Price	
		EF	*VF*
B248 **£1**	Pale blue (shades): "A" series		
	Prefix coding: Letter, number, number, letter.		
	Quantity printed: 297 million.		
	Width of design (i.e. signature block): 140–142 mm.		
	Serial letters:		
	A—D (series traced from A01D)	16·00	9·00
	A—E (series traced from A01E)	14·00	8·00
	A—H (series traced from A01H)	14·00	8·00
B249 **£1**	Blue (shades)		
	Prefix coding: Letter, number, number, letter		
	Width of design (i.e. signature block): 140–142 mm.		
	Quantity printed: 5148 million.		

B249

		Price	
		EF	*VF*

Serial letters:

B—D, C—D, D—D, E—D, H—D,
J—D, K—D, L—D, M—D, N—D,
O—D, R—D, S—D, T—D, U—D,

W—D, X—D, Y—D	*each*	8·00	4·00
Z—D (last series traced to Z86D)		14·00	8·00

B—E, C—E, D—E, E—E, H—E,
J—E, K—E, L—E, M—E, N—E,
O—E, R—E, S—E, T—E, U—E,

W—E (traced to W38E)	*each*	8·00	4·00
X—E, Y—E and Z—E (series not yet traced)		—	—

B—H, C—H, D—H, E—H, H—H,
J—H, K—H, L—H, M—H, N—H,
O—H, R—H, S—H, T—H, U—H,

W—H	*each*	8·00	4·00
X—H (traced to X94H)		14·00	8·00
Y—H and Z—H (series not yet traced)			

B250 £1 Blue replacement note
Prefix coding: Not known.
Quantity printed: Not known.
Serial letters: Not yet traced.

1940 (2 April) TEN SHILLINGS

The mauve emergency issue, incorporating a metal thread as the £1 above. Basic design and dimensions unchanged. Plate-printed until September 1940 at St. Luke's Works, London, on banknote paper manufactured by Portals Ltd. Thereafter by offset-litho at Overton, Hampshire. Emergency issue 10s. notes were legal tender until 29 October 1962.

B251

PEPPIATT (contd.)

Price
EF   VF

B251 **10s.** Mauve (shades)
Prefix coding: Letter, number, number, letter.
Width of design: 129 mm.
Quantity printed: 2200 million.
Serial letters:

		EF	VF
Z—D (first series traced from Z01D)		22·00	14·00
Y—D, X—D, W—D, U—D, T—D, S—D, R—D, O—D, N—D, M—D, L—D, K—D, J—D, H—D, E—D, D—D, C—D, B—D	*each*	16·00	9·00
A—D (last series traced to A99D)		20·00	12·00
Z—E (first series traced from Z01E)		20·00	12·00
Y—E		20·00	12·00
X—E (last series traced to X21E)		65·00	45·00

B252 **10s.** Mauve replacement note
Prefix coding: Not known.
Quantity printed: Not known.
Serial letters: Not yet traced.

For classification of specimen notes and errors, see page 149.

1941 (date unknown)

The emergency small-denomination notes of FIVE SHILLINGS and HALF-CROWN (signed K. O. Peppiatt) were prepared by the Bank of England on instructions from H.M. Government, who feared there might be difficulties in transporting coinage. The notes, which were printed on unwatermarked paper with the design on both sides, incorporate a metal thread, and measure 114 × 73 mm (4½ × 2⅞ in.). Although they were distributed to the clearing banks, the notes were never issued to the public and were destroyed in the late 1940s. Examples which have survived have no serial numbers.

B253

B254

			Price	
			EF	*VF*
B253 **5s.**	Olive-green (design) on pale pink (background)		£1500	£750

B253 **5s.** Olive-green (design) on pale pink
(background)
Prefix coding: None.
Widths of design and signature block:
98 mm and 104 mm.
Quantity printed: Not known.
Serial letters: None.

B254 **2s. 6d.** Black (design) on pale blue £1250 £750
(background)
Prefix coding: None.
Widths of design and signature block:
105 mm and 103 mm.
Quantity printed: Not known.
Serial letters: None.

1945 (18 October) FIVE POUNDS

Design, watermark and dimensions as for C. P. Mahon notes, but metal thread is now incorporated and all four edges are straight. The notes, which were printed at St. Luke's Works, London, were legal tender until 13 March 1961. (Although the notes were not issued until 1945, many of them bear dates from 1944 on.)

For prefix details *see* page 173.

B255 **£5** Black on white
Prefix coding: Letter, number, number.
Quantity printed: 40 million.
Serial letters:

E—(first series traced from E01 dated 2 September 1944)		48·00	28·00
H—, J—, K—	*each*	44·00	26·00
L—(last series traced to L02 dated 12 December 1945)		65·00	35·00

PEPPIATT (contd.)

THIRD PERIOD (1948)

1948 (17 June)

Re-issue of the unthreaded pre-war TEN SHILLINGS and ONE POUND notes. This enabled the Bank of England to use up stockpiled notes and supplies of paper without the metal thread. The design, dimensions and watermark were the same as for C. P. Mahon, but in the case of the £1 larger plates were used. The notes were printed at St. Luke's Works, London.

		Price	
		EF	VF

B256 **10s.** Red-brown
    Prefix coding: Number, number, letter.
    Width of design:
      Plate 1: 126 mm.
      Plate 2: 129 mm.
    Quantity printed: 65 million.
    Serial letter:
      —L (series traced from 05L to 71L)   45·00   25·00

B257 **10s.** Red-brown replacement note
    Prefix coding: Not known.
    Quantity printed: Not known.
    Serial letter: Not yet traced.

B256

B258

	Price	
	EF	*VF*

B258 **£1**   Green
      Prefix coding: Letter, number, number,
        letter.
      Width of design (i.e. signature block):
        141·5 mm.
      Quantity printed: 140 million.

      Serial letters:

	EF	VF
R—A (first traced from R01A)	28·00	18·00
S—A (last series traced to S48A)	32·00	19·00

Note—the serials of this issue overlap with those of the threaded £1
(B260).

B259 **£1**   Green replacement note
      Prefix coding: Letter, number, number,
        letter.
      Quantity printed: Not known.
      Serial letters: Not yet traced.

For classification of specimen notes and errors, *see* page 149.

PEPPIATT (contd.)

Fourth Period (1948–49)

1948 (13 September) One Pound

Design, watermark and dimensions as for C. P. Mahon, but metal thread is now incorporated and larger plates are used. Printed at St. Luke's Works, London.

B260 £1   Green

Prefix coding: Letter, number, number, letter.

Width of design (i.e. signature block):
Plate 1: 141·5 mm.
Plate 2: 143·5 mm.
Plate 3: 145 mm.

Quantity printed: 1190 million.

B260

	Price	
Serial letters:	EF	VF
S—A (first series traced from S39A)	28·00	16·00
T—A, U—A, W—A, X—A, Y—A *each*	12·00	8·00
Z—A (last series traced to Z99A)	14·00	9·00
A—B (first series traced from A01B)	14·00	9·00
B—B, C—B, D—B, E—B *each*	12·00	8·00
H—B (last series traced to H36B)	18·00	11·00

For plate 2 and plate 3 notes add 20% to the above prices.
Note—the serials of this issue overlap with those of the unthreaded £1 (B258).

B261 £1   Green replacement note

Prefix coding: Letter, number, number, letter.

Quantity printed: 9 million.

	Price	
	EF	*VF*

Serial letters:
   S—S (series traced from S01S to   £125   85·00
   S09S)

1948 (25 October) TEN SHILLINGS

Design, watermark and dimensions as for C. P. Mahon, but metal thread is now incorporated and larger plates are used for some notes. Printed at St. Luke's Works, London.

B262 10s. Red-brown
   Prefix coding: Number, number, letter.
   Width of design:
      Plate 1: 126 mm.
      Plate 2: 129 mm.
      Plate 3: 131 mm.
   Quantity printed: 420 million.
   Serial letters:

		EF	*VF*
—L (first series traced from 72L)		£125	85·00
—K, —J, —H	*each*	16·00	9·00
—E (last series traced to 91E)		22·00	14·00

For plate 1 notes add 25% to the above prices. For plate 3 notes add 50% to the above prices.

B262

B263 10s. Red-brown replacement note
   Prefix coding: Number, number, letter.
   Quantity printed: 3 million.
   Serial letter:
      —A (series traced from 01A to 03A)   £145   85·00

PEPPIATT (contd.)

1948 (9 September) FIVE POUNDS

Design, watermark and dimensions as for K. O. Peppiatt notes of Second Period (B255), but thin paper is used, and all notes are dated 1947. Printed at St. Luke's Works, London.
For prefix details *see* page 173.

		Price	
		EF	VF
B264 £5	Black on white		
	Prefix coding: Letter, number, number.		
	Quantity printed: Not known.		
	Serial letters:		
	L—(first series traced from L03	45·00	25·00
	dated 1 January 1947)		
	M—(last series traced to M71 dated	45·00	25·00
	16 July 1947)		

For classification of specimen notes and errors *see* page 149.

B264

Confusion has arisen over the identification of the four main types of Peppiatt notes. They are:

TEN SHILLINGS:
Type 1		Pre-war Letter, number, number (unthreaded)
Type 2a		Pre-war Number, number, letter (unthreaded)
	2b	Post-war Number, number, letter (unthreaded)
Type 3		Wartime Letter, number, number, letter (threaded)
Type 4		Post-war Number, number, letter (threaded)

ONE POUND:
Type 1		Pre-war Number, number, letter (unthreaded)
Type 2a		Pre-war Letter, number, number, letter (unthreaded)
	2b	Post-war Letter, number, number, letter (unthreaded)
Type 3		Wartime Letter, number, number, letter (threaded)
Type 4		Post-war Letter, number, number, letter (threaded)

Some notes on shading. St. Luke's Works, London was hit by two bombs on the night of 9/10 September 1940 and production of banknotes was then transferred to emergency premises near the Bank's paper suppliers, Portals, in Hampshire. Up to the move printing had been completed of the "A" serial £1 notes only. Although these notes have previously been distinguished by their pale blue colour, the same shades can be found in later issues. Students of shading may clearly identify at least 20 combinations of colour based on the following analysis:

Obverse main design	*Obverse background*
Pale blue	Pink
Blue	Deep pink
Deep blue (ultramarine)	Buff

Obverse signature block	*Reverse*
Light shading	Pale blue
Medium shading	Pale blue
Heavy shading	Greenish-blue

PEPPIATT (contd.)

B247

Percival Spencer Beale (1949–55)

Born 1906. Entered Bank service 1924. Chief Cashier 1 March 1949 to 16 January 1955.

1950 (17 March) TEN SHILLINGS

Design, watermark and dimensions as for K. O. Peppiatt notes of the Fourth Period. Printed at St. Luke's Works, London.

		Price	
		EF	*VF*

B265 10s. Red-brown
Prefix coding: Number, number, letter.
Width of design: 129 mm.
Quantity printed: 307 million.
Serial letters:

	Price EF	VF
—E (first series traced from 92E)	£125	85·00
—D, —C *each*	16·00	9·00
—B (last series traced to 99B)	16·00	9·00

B266 10s. Red-brown
Prefix coding: Letter, number, number, letter.
Width of design: 129 mm.
Quantity printed: 1668 million.
Serial letters:

	Price EF	VF
Z—Z (first series traced from Z01Z)	18·00	10·00
Y—Z, X—Z, W—Z, U—Z, T—Z, S—Z, R—Z, O—Z, N—Z, M—Z, L—Z, K—Z, J—Z, H—Z, E—Z *each*	12·00	8·00
D—Z (last series traced to D85Z)	22·00	12·00

B265

BEALE (contd.)

B266

	Price	
	EF	VF

B267 10s. Red-brown replacement note
Prefix coding: Number, number, letter.
Quantity printed: 30 million.
Serial letter:

	EF	VF
—A (series traced from 04A to 35A)	75·00	45·00

1950 (17 March) ONE POUND

Design, watermark and dimensions as for K. O. Peppiatt notes of the Fourth Period. Printed at St. Luke's Works, London.

B268 £1 Green
Prefix coding: Letter, number, number, letter.
Width of design (i.e. signature block);
141·5 mm.
Quantity printed: 4275 million.
Serial letters:

		EF	VF
H—B (first series traced from H37B)		14·00	8·00
J—B, K—B, L—B, M—B, N—B, O—B, R—B, S—B, T—B, U—B, W—B, X—B, Y—B	*each*	7·00	4·00
Z—B (last series traced to Z99B)		9·00	5·00
A—C (first series traced from A01C)		9·00	5·00
B—C, C—C, D—C, E—C, H—C, J—C, K—C, L—C, M—C, N—C, O—C, R—C, S—C, T—C, U—C, W—C, X—C, Y—C	*each*	7·00	4·00
Z—C (last series traced to Z99C)		9·00	5·00
A—J (first series traced from A01J)		9·00	5·00
B—J, C—J, D—J, E—J, H—J, J—J, K—J	*each*	7·00	4·00
L—J (last series traced to L63J)		12·00	8·00

B269

	Price	
	EF	VF

B269 £1 Green replacement note
Prefix coding: Letter, number, number,
letter.
Quantity printed: 60 million
Serial letters:
    S—S (series traced from S10S to   38·00   20·00
    S70S)

1949 (13 December) FIVE POUNDS

Design, watermark and dimensions as for K. O. Peppiatt notes of the
Second Period (B255). Printed at St. Luke's Works, London.
For prefix details *see* page 173.

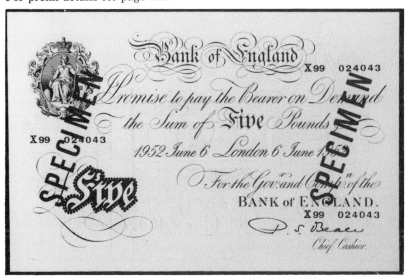

B270

| | Price | |
| | *EF* | *VF* |

B270 **£5**   Black on white
        Prefix coding: Letter, number, number.
        Quantity printed: Not known.
        Serial letters:

M—(first series traced from M72 dated 1 March 1949)		45·00	25·00
N—, O—, P—, R—, S—, T—, U—, V—, W—, X—	*each*	40·00	22·00
Y— (last series traced to Y70 dated 27 August 1952)		45·00	25·00

For classification of specimen notes and errors *see* page 149.

SERIES B (HELMETED BRITANNIA) UNISSUED

It should not be thought that the Bank of England were lacking in ideas for designs to replace the 1928 issue. In June 1931, Kruger Gray, Frederick Griggs and Stephen Gooden were invited to compete for new note designs, although Gooden's winning entry was not printed.

During the 1930s Gooden completed a number of other designs for 10s. and £1 notes, including a 10s. featuring St. George and the Dragon and a £1 note showing a bare headed Britannia holding a spear.

Then in the late 1940s and early 1950s Gooden produced two further series of notes: one of these depicted Sir John Houblon, first governor of the Bank and was known as the "Houblon" series. The series selected for issue was officially designated Series B and depicted on the obverse a vignette of Britannia helmeted. The reverses of the three denominations, 10s., £1 and £5 showed three variations of a lion and key motif on multicoloured background.

Copyright Bank of England

Gooden himself did not live to see the issue of the £5 in February 1957 (with the signature of O'Brien). This note was already in production when it was announced in July 1956 that H.M. The Queen had consented to her portrait appearing on Bank of England notes. As a result plans to bring in the Series B 10s. and £1 were shelved, and Gooden's successor Robert Austin set to work on the Series C (portrait) notes.

Copyright Bank of England

Copyright Bank of England

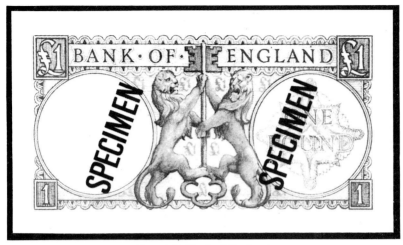

Copyright Bank of England

Notes: For further information see "In Search of Stephen Gooden" by John Deacon in *The Old Lady of Threadneedle Street*, September 1980. Also "The Search For the 'Inimitable' Note" by Clive Goodacre in *Penrose* 1982 (International Review of the Graphic Arts). The latter also contains much of interest relating to the Series D (Pictorial) notes 1970–1981.

Leslie Kenneth O'Brien (1955–62)

Born 1908. Entered Bank service 1927. Chief Cashier 1955. Director 1962–64. Deputy Governor 1964–66. Governor 1966–73. First member of the bank's ordinary staff to become Governor. Knighted 1967 and became Lord O'Brien of Lothbury in 1973.

First (Britannia) Period (1955–60)

1955 (21 November) Ten Shillings

Design, watermark and dimensions as for K. O. Peppiatt notes of the Fourth Period. Printed at St. Luke's Works, London.

		Price	
		EF	*VF*
B271 10s. Red-brown			
Prefix coding: Letter, number, number, letter.			
Width of design: 129 mm.			
Quantity printed: 2500 million.			
Serial letters:			
D—Z (first series traced from D86Z)		35·00	22·00
C—Z, B—Z		12·00	8·00
A—Z (last series traced to A95Z)		14·00	9·00
Z—Y (first series traced from Z01Y)		16·00	10·00
Y—Y, X—Y, W—Y, U—Y, T—Y, S—Y, R—Y, O—Y, N—Y, M—Y, L—Y, K—Y, J—Y, H—Y, E—Y, D—Y, C—Y, B—Y	*each*	10·00	7·00
A—Y (last series traced to A99Y)		14·00	9·00
Z—X (first series traced from Z02X)		15·00	10·00
Y—X (last series traced to Y25X)		24·00	14·00

B271

B272

	Price	
	EF	VF

B272 **10s.** Red-brown replacement note
Prefix coding: Number, number, letter.
Quantity printed: 32 million.
Serial letters:

—A (series traced from 36A to 68A)	55·00	35·00

1955 (21 November) ONE POUND

Design, watermark and dimensions as for K. O. Peppiatt notes of the Fourth Period. Printed at St. Luke's Works, London.

B273 **£1** Green
Prefix coding: Letter, number, number, letter.
Width of design (i.e. signature block): 141·5 mm.
Quantity printed: 3900 million.
Serial letters:

		EF	VF
L—J (first series traced from L64J)		12·00	8·00
M—J, N—J, O—J, R—J, S—J, T—J, U—J, W—J, X—J, Y—J	*each*	6·00	4·00
Z—J (last series traced to Z99J)		8·00	4·00
A—K (first series traced from A01K)		8·00	4·00
B—K, C—K, D—K, E—K, H—K, J—K, K—K, L—K, M—K, N—K, O—K, R—K, S—K, T—K, U—K, W—K, X—K, Y—K	*each*	6·00	4·00
Z—K (last series traced to Z99K)		8·00	4·00
A—L (first series traced from A01L)		8·00	4·00
B—L, C—L, D—L, E—L, H—L, J—L	*each*	6·00	4·00
K—L (last series traced to K13L)		35·00	22·00

O'BRIEN (contd.)

B273

		Price
	EF	*VF*

B274 £1 Green replacement note
Prefix coding: Letter, number, number,
letter.
Quantity printed: 51 million.
Serial letters:

	EF	VF
S—S (series traced from S71S to S99S)	40·00	22·00
S—T (series traced from S01T to S22T)	45·00	25·00

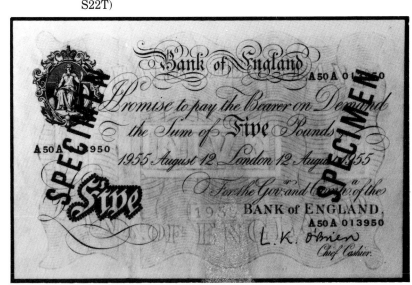

B276

1955 (5 July) Five Pounds

Design, watermark and dimensions as for K. O. Peppiatt notes of the Second period (B255). Printed at St. Luke's Works, London.
For prefix details *see* page 174.

			Price	
			EF	*VF*
B275 **£5**	Black on white			
	Prefix coding: Letter, number, number.			
	Quantity printed: Not known.			
	Serial letters:			
	Y— (first series traced from Y71			
	dated 17 January 1955)		60·00	30·00
	Z—(last series traced to Z99 dated 15			
	June 1955.		50·00	28·00
B276 **£5**	Black on white			
	Prefix coding: Letter, number, number,			
	letter.			
	Quantity printed: Not known.			
	Serial letters:			
	A—A (first series traced from A01A			
	dated 16 June 1955)		48·00	26·00
	B—A, C—A	*each*	43·00	25·00
	D—A (last series traced to D99A			
	dated 20 September 1956)		48·00	26·00

SERIES B 1957–67

1957 (21 February) FIVE POUNDS

Designed by Stephen Gooden R.A. featuring on the obverse the helmeted head of Britannia, and on the reverse the lion and key (for details of the series see page 103). Plate-printed in sheets of 21 at St. Luke's Works, London, on banknote paper manufactured by Portals Ltd. with watermark incorporating the helmeted head of Britannia. (Britannia) Five Pound notes measure 160 × 90 mm (6¼ × 3½ in.) and were legal tender until 27 June 1967.

		Price	
		EF	*VF*
B277 **£5**	Blue, pale green and orange		
	Prefix coding: Letter, number, number.		
	Quantity printed: 450 million.		
	Serial letters:		
	A—(first series traced from A01)	20·00	14·00
	B—, C—, D—, E—	16·00	12·00
	H—(last series traced to H67)	20·00	14·00
B278 **£1**	Multicoloured (Blue and lilac predominating) Never issued.	–	–
B279 **10s.**	Multicoloured (Purple and orange predominating) Never issued.	–	–

1961 (12 July) FIVE POUNDS

Design, watermark and dimensions as B277 above, except that the £5 symbols on the reverse are printed in outline only instead of shaded in dark blue. Printed at the Bank of England Works, Loughton, Essex.

B280 **£5** Blue, pale green and orange
Prefix coding: Letter, number, number
Quantity printed: 200 million.

B277/279

	Price	
	EF	*VF*
Serial letters:		
H—(first series traced from H20)	20·00	14·00
J—	18·00	13·00
K—(last series traced to K45)	20·00	14·00

It will be noticed that serial numbers of B277 and B279 overlap in the H— series.

Reverse of B277

Reverse of B280

SERIES C (PORTRAIT) 1960–1979

Stephen Gooden died on 21 September 1955 and was replaced by Robert Austin, R.A. Professor of Engraving at the Royal College of Art, and President of both the Royal Society of Painters in Water-Colours and the Royal Society of Painter-Etchers and Engravers.

In July 1956 it was announced that H.M. The Queen had consented to her portrait appearing on Bank of England notes; on 19 November 1959 the Bank announced that the new £1 note bearing for the first time a portrait of the reigning monarch, would be issued in 1960. The new series was to have denominations up to £10.

The £1 and 10s. notes which were designed by Robert Austin, incorporate the Queen's portrait in a complex blend of machine-engraved geometric patterns, and on the reverse, the figure of Britannia seated. The notes were initially printed (by the intaglio process) in sheets of 24 at the Bank of England Works, Loughton, Essex, on banknote paper manufactured by Portals Ltd., with watermark of continuous laureate head. However, in 1961, experimental notes were produced on a new reel-fed web press, developed in conjunction with the Bank's own engineers by Masson, Scott, Thrissell Engineering Ltd, of Bristol. To identify them from other notes in circulation, they carried the serial prefixes A01N, A05N and A06N together with the small capital letter "R" (standing for Research) on the reverse (*see* B283).

Portrait £1 notes (the usual term used by collectors) measure 151 × 72 mm (6 × 2¾ in.) and were legal tender until 31 May 1979. The portrait 10s. notes measure 140 × 66 mm (5½ × 2⅝ in.) and were legal tender until 22 November 1970.

B281

1960 (17 March) ONE POUND

Design, watermark and dimensions as detailed above.

Price
EF   *VF*

B281 **£1**   Green
          Prefix coding: Letter, number, number.
          Quantity printed: 1782 million.

			Price	
			EF	*VF*
Serial letters:				
A—(first series traced from A01)			9·00	4·00
B—, C—, D—, E—, H—, J—, K—,				
L—, N—, R—, S—, T—, U—, W—,				
X—, Y—	*each*		6·00	4·00
Z—(last series traced to Z99)			9·00	4·00

B282 £1 Green
Prefix coding: Number, number, letter.
Quantity printed: 1782 million.

Serial letters:				
—A (first series traced from 01A)			9·00	4·00
—B, —C, —D, —E, —H, —J, —K, —L,				
—N, —R, —S, —T, —U, —W, —X,				
—Y	*each*		6·00	4·00
—Z (last series traced to 99Z)			9·00	4·00

B283 £1 Green
Prefix coding: Letter, number, number,
 letter ("R" reverse).
Quantity printed: 6 million (3 million
 issued)
Serial letters:
 A—N (series traced in A01N, A05N
 and A06N only)   £145   75·00

Common reverse of £1 O'Brien to Page

Notes with A01N have a long tail to the "R", whereas those with A05N and A06N have a short-tailed "R". So far no trace has been found of notes with the prefix A02N, A03N and A04N, which were printed but not put into general circulation.

O'BRIEN (contd.)

B284 **£1**   Green
         Prefix coding: Letter, number, number,
            letter.
         Quantity printed: 76 million.
         Serial letters:
            B—N (series traced from B01N to
            B76N)   18·00   10·00

B285 **£1**   Green replacement note
         Prefix coding: Letter, number, number.
         Quantity printed: 66 million.
         Serial letter:
            M—(series traced from M01 to M68)   15·00   9·00

B283 showing position of "R" on reverse. The "G" variety found
on B292 and subsequent notes is also in this position.

B286

1961 (12 October) TEN SHILLINGS

Design, watermark and dimensions as detailed above.

B286 **10s.**   Red-brown
         Prefix coding: Letter, number, number.
         Quantity printed: 756 million.

	Price	
	EF	*VF*

Serial letters:
    A—(first series traced from A01)   9·00   5·00

    B—, C—, D—, E—, H—, J—   *each*   7·00   4·00

    K—(last series traced to K64)   12·00   8·00

B287 **10s.** Red-brown replacement note
    Prefix coding: Letter, number, number.
    Quantity printed: 18 million.
    Serial letter:
        M—(series traced from M01 to M18)   35·00   20.00

The £5 notes of this period (B277 and B280) can be found on page 110. For classification of specimen notes and errors *see* page 149.

Reverse of B286

Jasper Quintus Hollom (1962–66)

Born 1917. Entered Bank service 1936. Chief Cashier 1 March 1962 to 30 June 1966. Director from 1966. Deputy Governor 1970. Knighted 1975.

1963 (27 February) ONE POUND

Design, watermark and dimensions as for L. K. O'Brien portrait notes. Plate-printed at the Bank of England Works, Loughton, Essex. Some notes (B292 and 293) carrying the small capital letter "G" on the reverse, were printed on a reel fed German Goebel press which the Bank used experimentally in the early 1960s.

B288

B295

				Price	
				EF	*VF*
B288 £1	Green				
	Prefix coding: Letter, number, number, letter.				
	Quantity printed: 5875 million.				
	Serial letters:				
	B—N (first series traced from B77N)			40·00	25·00
	C—N, D—N, E—N, H—N, J—N,				
	K—N, L—N		*each*	7·00	4·00
	A—R, B—R, C—R, D—R, E—R,				
	H—R, J—R, K—R, L—R		*each*	7·00	4·00

		Price	
		EF	*VF*
A—S, B—S, C—S, D—S, E—S, H—S, J—S, K—S, L—S	*each*	7·00	4·00
A—T, B—T, C—T, E—T, H—T, J—T, K—T, L—T	*each*	7·00	4·00
A—U, B—U, C—U, D—U, E—U, H—U, J—U, K—U, L—U	*each*	7·00	4·00
A—W, B—W, D—W, E—W, H—W, J—W, K—W, L—W	*each*	7·00	4·00
A—X, B—X, C—X, D—X, E—X, H—X, J—X, K—X	*each*	7·00	4·00
A—Y	*each*	7·00	4·00
B—Y (last series traced to B11Y)		35·00	22·00

B289 £1 Green replacement note
Prefix coding: Letter, number, number.
Quantity printed: 32 million.
Serial letter:
M—(series traced from M68 to M99) 24·00 14·00

B290 £1 Green replacement note
Prefix coding: Number, number, letter.
Quantity printed: 99 million.
Serial letter:
—M(series traced from 01M to 99M) 15·00 9·00

B291 £1 Green replacement note
Prefix coding: Letter, number, number, letter.
Quantity printed: 8 million.
Serial letters:
M—R (series traced from M01R to M08R) 16·00 10·00

B292 £1 Green (printed on a Goebel machine)
Prefix coding: Letter, number, number, letter ("G" reverse; *see* illustration page 114).
Quantity printed: 387 million.
Serial letters:
A—N (first series traced from A09N) 12·00 7·00
D—T,
C—W, 7·00 4·00
L—X (last series traced to L99X)

B293 £1 Green replacement note (printed on a Goebel machine)
Prefix coding: Letter, number, number, letter ("G" reverse).
Quantity printed: 28 million.

HOLLOM (contd.)

B297/298

Reverse of B297/298

	Price	
	EF	*VF*
Serial letters:		
M—N (series traced from M01N to M28N)	16·00	10·00

1963 (4 April) TEN SHILLINGS

Design, watermark and dimensions as for L. K. O'Brien portrait notes
Printed at the Bank of England Works, Loughton, Essex.

B294 **10s.** Red-brown
    Prefix coding: Letter, number, number.
    Quantity printed: 1025 million.
    Serial letters:

K—(first series traced from K65)		12·00	8·00
L—, N—, R—, S—, T—, U—, W—, X—, Y—	*each*	6·00	3·00
Z—(last series traced to Z99)		9·00	5·00

		Price	
		EF	*VF*

B295 10s. Red-brown
Prefix coding: Number, number, letter.
Quantity printed: 1015 million.
Serial letters:

—A (first series traced from 01A)		9·00	5·00
—B, —C, —D, —E, —H, —J, —K,			
—L, —N	*each*	6·00	3·00
—R (last series traced to 26R)		25·00	14·00

B296 10s. Red-brown replacement note
Prefix coding: Letter, number, number.
Quantity printed: 34 million.
Serial letter:

M—(series traced from M19 to M55)	32·00	22·00

1963 (21 February) FIVE POUNDS

Designed by Reynolds Stone, C.B.E., R.D.I., and of similar appearance to the £1 and 10s. notes, featuring the Queen's portrait on the obverse, and the figure of a child Britannia (modelled by the artist's daughter) on the reverse. Plate-printed in sheets of 21 at the Bank of England Works, Loughton, Essex, on banknote paper manufactured by Portals Ltd., with watermark of a continuous laureate head. Portrait £5 notes measure 140 × 84 mm (5½ × 3⁵/₁₆ in.) and were legal tender until 31 August 1973.

B297 £5 Blue
Prefix coding: Letter, number, number.
Quantity printed: 1007 million.
Serial letters:

A—(first series traced from A01)		20·00	14·00
B—, C—, D—, E—, H—, J—, K—,			
L—, N—	*each*	16·00	12·00
R— (last series traced to R16)		28·00	18·00

B298 £5 Blue replacement note
Prefix coding: Letter, number, number.
Quantity printed: 16 million.
Serial letter:

M—(series traced from M01 to M16)	48·00	38·00

1964 (21 February) TEN POUNDS

Designed by Reynolds Stone, C.B.E., R.D.I., featuring the Queen's portrait on the obverse together with a figure of Britannia seated; and on the reverse a lion holding a key with the words "Ten Pounds" in a scroll issuing from its mouth. Plate-printed in sheets of 15 at the Bank of England Works, Loughton, Essex, on banknote paper manufactured by Portals Ltd., with watermark of the Queen's head. Portrait £10 notes measure 150 × 93 mm (5⅞ × 3⅝ in.) and were legal tender until 31 May 1979.

HOLLOM (contd.)   *Price*
                                                      EF   VF

B299 **£10**   Brown
               Prefix coding: Letter, number, number.
               Quantity printed: 40 million.
               Serial letter:
                   A—(series traced from A01 to A40)   28·00   18·00

B299 common reverse of £10 between Hollom and Page

B300 **£10**   Brown replacement note
               Prefix coding: Letter, number, number.
               Quantity printed: Not known.
               Serial letter:
                   M—(series thought to exist in M01)   –   –

For classification of specimen notes and errors *see* page 149.

> ### John Standish Fforde (1966–70)

Born 1921. Entered Bank service 1957. Chief Cashier 1 July 1966 to 28 February 1970. Director 1970.

1967 (15 February) ONE POUND

Design, watermark and dimensions as for L. K. O'Brien portrait notes. Plate-printed at the Bank of England Works, Loughton, Essex. Some notes (B303, B304, B307 and B308) carry a small capital letter "G" on the reverse indicating that they were printed on an experimental German Goebel press. By the mid 1970s the Bank had installed four Masson, Scott, Thrissell web presses on which all £1 notes were being printed. By 1968 the existing serial letter combinations (using the second half of the alphabet N to Z as the control) had been exhausted so the Bank started to use the first half of the alphabet as the control letter (N—A, R—A, S—A and so on).

B301

			Price	
			EF	*VF*
B301 £1	Green			
	Prefix coding: Letter, number, number, letter (type 1).			
	Quantity printed: 1475 million.			
	Serial letters:			
	B—Y (first series traced from B11Y)		28·00	18·00
	C—Y, D—Y, H—Y, J—Y, K—Y, L—Y	*each*	6·00	3·00
	A—Z, B—Z, C—Z, D—Z, E—Z, H—Z, J—Z, L—Z	*each*	6·00	3·00
B302 £1	Green replacement note			
	Prefix coding: Letter, number, number, letter (type 1).			

FFORDE (contd.)

			Price	
			EF	*VF*

Quantity printed: 38 million.
Serial letters:
  M—R (series traced from M09R to
  M49R)   14·00   9·00

B303 £1 Green (printed on a Goebel machine)
Prefix coding: Letter, number, number,
  letter (type 1) ("G" reverse)
Quantity printed: 198 million.
Serial letters:
  E—Y, K—Z   *each*   7·00   4·00

B304 £1 Green replacement note (printed on a
  Goebel machine)
Prefix coding: Letter, number, number,
  letter (type 1) ("G" reverse).
Quantity printed: 14 million.
Serial letters:
  M—N (series traced from M29N to
  M42N)   30·00   18·00

B305 £1 Green
Prefix coding: Letter, number, number,
  letter (type 2).
Quantity printed: 4000 million
  (estimated).
Serial letters:

		EF	*VF*
N—A (first series traced from N01A)		7·00	4·00
N—B, N—C, N—D, N—E, N—H, N—J, N—K, N—L	*each*	5·00	2·00
R—A, R—C, R—D, R—E, R—H, R—J, R—K	*each*	5·00	2·00
S—A, S—B, S—C, S—D, S—E, S—H, S—J, S—K, S—L	*each*	5·00	2·00
T—A, T—B, T—C, T—D, T—E, T—H, T—J, T—K, T—L	*each*	5·00	2·00
U—A, U—B, U—C, U—D	*each*	5·00	2·00
W—A, W—B, W—C	*each*	5·00	2·00
X—B, X—C (last series traced to X41C)	*each*	5·00	2·00

B306 £1 Green replacement note
Prefix coding: Letter, number, number,
  letter (type 2).
Quantity printed: 300 million
  (estimated).
Serial letters:

		EF	*VF*
R—M (series traced from R01M)		14·00	9·00
S—M, U—M	*each*	12·00	8·00
T—M		48·00	35·00

£1 notes bearing the signatures of J. S. Fforde and J. B. Page with consecutive serial numbers are available (EF) at £60 a pair.

			Price	
			EF	VF
B307 £1	Green (printed on a Goebel machine) *Prefix coding:* Letter, number, number, letter (type 2). *Quantity printed:* 250 million (estimated). *Serial letters:* R—B, R—L, U—E	*each*	6·00	3·00
B308 £1	Green replacement note (Printed on a Goebel machine) *Prefix coding:* Letter, number, number, letter (type 2). *Quantity printed:* 100 million (estimated). *Serial letters:* N—M		15·00	8·00
	T—M		45·00	35·00

Note—the T—M prefix has been traced without the "G" reverse from T01M to T04M; and with "G" reverse from T29M to T32M. Both are rare.

1967 (15 February) TEN SHILLINGS

Design, watermark and dimensions as for L. K. O'Brien notes of the Second Period. Printed at the Bank of England Works, Loughton, Essex.

B309 10s.	Red-brown *Prefix coding:* Number, number, letter. *Quantity printed:* 768 million. *Serial letters:* —R (first series traced from 26R)		12·00	8·00
	—S, —T, —U, —W, —X, —Y	*each*	4·00	2·00
	—Z (last series traced to 99Z)		7·00	4·00
B310 10s.	Red-brown *Prefix coding:* Letter, number, number, letter. *Quantity printed:* 335 million. *Serial letters:* A—N (first series traced from A01N). B—N, C—N, D—N (last series traced to D38N)	*each*	5·00	2·00
B311 10s	Red-brown replacement note *Prefix coding:* Letter, number, number. *Quantity printed:* 25 million. *Serial letters:* M—(series traced from M56 to M80)		10·00	5·00

FFORDE (contd.)

B310

1967 (9 January) FIVE POUNDS

Design, watermark and dimensions as for J. Q. Hollom notes. Printed at the Bank of England Works, Loughton.

		Price	
		EF	*VF*
B312 **£5**	Blue		
	Prefix coding: Letter, number, number.		
	Quantity printed: 775 million.		
	Serial letters:		
	R—(first series traced from R20)	24·00	16·00
	S—, T—, U—, W—, X—, Y—, Z—		
	(last series traced to Z99) *each*	15·00	11·00
B313 **£5**	Blue replacement note		
	Prefix coding: Letter, number, number.		
	Quantity printed: 23 million.		
	Serial letters:		
	M—(series traced from M15 to M38)	45·00	35·00
B314 **£5**	Blue		
	Prefix coding: Number, number, letter.		
	Quantity printed: 850 million		
	(including B323).		
	Serial letters:		
	—A (first series traced from 01A)	19·00	13·00
	—B, —C, —D, —E, —H, —J, —K *each*	15·00	11·00
	—L (last series traced to 40L)	24·00	16·00
B315 **£5**	Blue replacement note		
	Prefix coding: Number, number, letter.		
	Quantity printed: 15 million (including		
	B324)		
	Serial letters:		
	—M (series traced from 01M to 15M)	45·00	35·00

B314

£5 notes bearing the signatures of J. S. Fforde and J. B. Page with consecutive serial numbers are available (EF) at £75 a pair.

1967 (9 January) TEN POUNDS

Design, watermark and dimensions as for J. Q. Hollom notes. Printed at the Bank of England Works, Loughton.

		EF	*VF*
		Price	

B316 **£10** Brown
Prefix coding: Letter, number, number.
Quantity printed: 50 million.
Serial letters:
A—(series traced from A41 to A95)   26·00   16·00

B317 **£10** Brown replacement note
Prefix coding: Letter, number, number.
Quantity printed: under 1 million.
Serial letters:
M—(series traced in M01 only)   65·00   30·00

£10 notes bearing the signatures of J. S. Fforde and J. B. Page with consecutive serial numbers are available (EF) at £95 a pair.

B316

FFORDE (contd.)

B318

Reverse of B318, 319, 329, 329, 347 (common design)

For Fforde £20 note see series D (Pictorial), page 127.

SERIES D (PICTORIAL) 1970—PRESENT DAY

The present Pictorial series of £50, £20, £10, £5 and £1 notes is the work of Harry Eccleston, assisted by Roger Withington and David Wicks. Eccleston joined the bank in 1958 and later became the first full time banknote designer. By the time the £50 note was issued in 1981, nearly 12 years work had gone into the series which broke much new ground in design and production.

1970 (9 July) TWENTY POUNDS

Designed by Harry Eccleston featuring on the obverse the Queen's portrait with a vignette of St. George and the dragon; the reverse shows the statue of Shakespeare from the Kent Memorial in Westminster Abbey and a scene from *Romeo and Juliet*. Plate-printed in sheets of 15 at the Bank of England Works, Loughton, Essex, on banknote paper manufactured by Portals Ltd. with watermark of the Queen's head. Twenty pound notes measure 160 × 90 mm (6⁵/₁₆ × 3 ⁹/₁₆ in.) and are still legal tender. Although the first issue of the notes was signed by J. S. Fforde, he had, in fact, ceased to be Chief Cashier four months previously in March 1970.

			Price	
			EF	VF
B318	£20	Multicoloured (purple predominating) *Prefix coding:* Letter, number, number. *Quantity printed:* 5 million. *Serial letters:*		
		A—(series traced from A01 to A05)	58·00	38·00
B319	£20	Multicoloured replacement note *Prefix coding:* Letter, number, number. *Quantity printed:* Fewer than 1 million. *Serial letters:*		
		M—(series traced in M01 only)	75·00	45·00

For classification of specimen notes and errors *see* page 149.

John Brangwyn Page (1970–1980)

Born 1924. Entered Bank service 1948. Assistant Chief Cashier 1966. First deputy Chief Cashier 1968. Chief Cashier 1 March 1970 to 29 February 1980, Director 1980.

SERIES C

1971 (date unknown) ONE POUND

Design, watermark and dimensions as for L. K. O'Brien portrait notes. Printed from plates or on continuous reel-fed machines at the Bank of England Works, Loughton, Essex. (£1 notes bearing the signature of J. B. Page were issued concurrently with those of J. S. Fforde for two years with many serial prefixes shared by both cashiers.)

		Price	
		EF	*VF*
B320 **£1**	Green		
	Prefix coding: Letter, number, number, letter.		
	Quantity printed: 3900 million (estimated).		
	Serial letters:		
	S—L (first series, traced in S87L, S89L and S90L only)	25·00	14·00
	T—B, T—D, T—E, T—H, T—K, T—L		
	U—A, U—B, U—C, U—D, U—H		
	W—A, W—B, W—C, W—D, W—E, W—H		
	X—A, X—B, X—C, X—D, X—E, X—H, X—J, X—K, X—L	*each* 4·00	2·00
	Y—A, Y—B, Y—C, Y—D, Y—E, Y—H, Y—J, Y—K, Y—L		
	Z—A, Z—B, Z—C, Z—D, Z—E, Z—H, Z—J, Z—K		
	Z—L	7·00	4·00

B320

			Price	
			EF	*VF*
B321 £1	Green replacement note			
	Prefix coding: Letter, number, number, letter.			
	Quantity printed: 300 million.			
	Serial letters:			
	R—M (first series traced from R44M)		13·00	8·00
	S—M, W—M		10·00	6·00
	X—M (last series traced to X60M)		10·00	6·00

£1 notes with consecutive serial numbers bearing the signatures of J. B. Page and J. S. Fforde are available EF at £60 a pair.

By mid-1973, the existing serial combinations were almost used up, and the Bank of England introduced the serial prefix letter, letter, number, number for the first time. From 1974 all £1 notes were printed on reel-fed web presses.

B322 £1	Green			
	Prefix coding: Letter, letter, number, number.			
	Quantity printed: 4715 million.			
	Serial letters:			
	AN—(first series traced from AN01)		8·00	4·00
	AR—, AS—, AT—, AU—, AW—, AX—, AY—, AZ—			
	BN—, BR—, BS—, BT—, BU—, BW—, BX—, BY—, BZ—			
	CN—, CR—, CS—, CT—, CU—, CW—, CX—, CY—, CZ—			
	DN—, DR—, DS—, DT—, DU—, DW—, DX—, DY—, DZ—	*each*	4.00	2.00
	EN—, ER—, ES—, ET—, EU—, EW—, EX—, EY—, EZ—			
	HN—, HR—, HS—, HT—, HU—, HW—, HX—, HY—			
	HZ—(last series traced to HZ62)		8·00	4·00
B323 £1	Green replacement note			
	Prefix coding: Letter, letter, number, number.			
	Quantity printed: 415 million.			
	Serial letters:			
	MR—(first series traced from MR01) MS—, MT—, MU— MW—(last series traced to MW19)	*each*	7·00	4·00

PAGE (contd.)

B322

1971 (date unknown) FIVE POUNDS

Design, watermark and dimensions as for J. Q. Hollom notes. Printed at the Bank of England Works, Loughton, Essex. (Five pound notes bearing the signature of J. B. Page were issued concurrently with those of J. S. Fforde for two years with some serial prefixes shared by both cashiers.)

		Price	
		EF	*VF*
B324 **£5**	Blue		
	Prefix coding: Number, number, letter.		
	Quantity printed: 550 million (including B314)		
	Serial letters:		
	—C (first series traced from 26C)	22·00	12·00
	—D, —E, —H, —J, —K	17·00	10·00
	—L (last series traced to 30L)	22·00	12·00

B324

B325 **£5**   Blue replacement note
        Prefix coding: Number, number, letter
        Quantity printed: 15 million (including
         B315)
        Serial letters:
        —M (series traced from 04M to 14M)   45·00   35·00

£5 notes bearing the signatures of J. B. Page and J. S. Fforde with consecutive serial numbers are available (EF) at £60 a pair.

1971 (date unknown) TEN POUNDS

Design, watermark and dimensions as for J. Q. Hollom notes. Printed at the Bank of England Works, Loughton, Essex.

B326 **£10**   Brown
        Prefix coding: Letter, number, number.
        Quantity printed: 350 million.
        Serial letters:
        A—(first series traced from A92)   65·00   35·00
        B—, C—, D—   *each*   24·00   18·00
        E—   48·00   28·00

B327 **£10**   Brown replacement note
        Prefix coding: Letter, number, number.
        Quantity printed: 17 million.
        Serial letters:
        M—(series traced M01 to M17)   32·00   16·00

£10 notes bearing the signatures of J. B. Page and J. S. Fforde with consecutive serial numbers are available (EF) at £85 a pair.
For classification of specimen notes and errors *see* page 149.

B326

SERIES D (PICTORIAL)

For design details etc; *see* page 127.

1970 (date not known) TWENTY POUNDS

Design, dimensions and watermark as for J. S. Fforde notes. Printed at the Bank of England Works, Loughton.

			Price	
			EF	*VF*
B328	**£20**	Multicoloured (purple predominating) *Prefix coding:* Letter, number, number. *Quantity printed:* 300 million. *Serial letters:*		
		A—(first series traced from A06)	50·00	34·00
		B—, C—	48·00	32·00
		D—(last series traced to D10)	50·00	34·00
B329	**£20**	Multicoloured replacement note *Prefix coding:* Letter, number, number. *Quantity printed:* 1 million. *Serial letters:*		
		M—(first series traced in M01 and M02 only)	65·00	38·00

B329

1975 (20 February) TEN POUNDS

Designed by Harry Eccleston as the third in the series D (Pictorial) notes. The obverse features the Queen's portrait in State Robes, a medallion of Britannia and a vignette derived from the lily symbol used by Florence Nightingale. On the reverse the portrait of Florence Nightingale was created from photographs taken on her return from the Crimean War. It is set beside a vignette based on a contemporary lithograph showing her at work in the Barracks Hospital, Scutari. Plate-printed in sheets of 20 at the Bank of England Works, Loughton, Essex, on banknote paper manufac-

PAGE (contd.)

tured by Portals Ltd., with watermark of Florence Nightingale's head. These notes measure 151 × 84·87 mm (5⅞ × 3⁵⁄₁₆ in.) and are still legal tender.

		Price	
		EF	*VF*
B330 **£10**	Multicoloured (brown predominating)		
	Prefix coding: Letter, number, number.		
	Quantity printed: 980 million.		
	Serial letters:		
	A—(first series traced from A01)	28·00	18·00
	B—, C—, D—, E—, H—, K—, L—,		
	N—, R—, S—	23·00	17·00
	T—(last series traced to T20)	28·00	18·00
B331 **£10**	Multicoloured replacement note		
	Prefix coding: Letter, number, number.		
	Quantity printed: 10 million.		
	Serial letters:		
	M—(series traced from M01 to M10)	30·00	20·00

B330

Reverse of B330

1971 (11 November) FIVE POUNDS

Designed by Harry Eccleston as the second of the Pictorial series of notes.
On the obverse it features the Queen's portrait, a medallion of Britannia
and a vignette depicting a Winged Victory, a symbol of military prowess.
On the reverse there is a portrait of the first Duke of Wellington and a
vignette of a scene based on a 19th century engraving of the Battle of
Fuentes de Onoro which took place in 1811 during the Peninsular War.
Initially plate-printed in sheets of 18 at the Bank of England Works,
Loughton, Essex, on banknote paper manufactured by Portals Ltd., with
continuous watermark of Wellington's head. Pictorial £5 notes measure
145·5 × 77·8 mm (5¾ × 3¹/₁₆ in.) and are still legal tender. From 1973 £5
notes were printed on the web presses, intaglio on the front and offset litho
on the back. The new notes used different serial prefixes and had a small
capital "L" on the reverse (standing for Litho).

		Price	
		EF	VF
B332 **£5**	Multicoloured (pale blue predominating) *Prefix coding:* Letter, number, number. *Quantity printed:* 810 million. *Serial letters:*		
	A—(first series traced from A01)	20·00	11·00
	B—, C—, D—, E—, H—, J—, K— *each*	15·00	9·00
	L—(last series traced to L90)	22·00	12·00
B333 **£5**	Multicoloured replacement note *Prefix coding:* Letter, number, number. *Quantity printed:* 4 million. *Serial letters:*		
	M—(series traced from M01 to M04)	40·00	22·00

B332/336 (common design)

PAGE (contd.)

Reverse of B332/333

1973 (August) FIVE POUNDS

Design, dimensions and watermark as for B332 above, but note carries small capital letter "L" on the reverse to the right of the £5 denomination, to indicate it was printed by lithography. It is also distinguished by a different serial prefix: Number, number, letter.

		Price	
		EF	*VF*

B334 **£5**   Multicoloured (pale blue predominating)

    Prefix coding: Number, number, letter.
    Quantity printed: 1600 million.
    Serial letters:

	EF	*VF*
—A (first series traced from 01A)	20·00	11·00
—B, —C, —D, —E, —H, —J, —K, —L, —N, —R, —S, —T, —U, —W, —X, —Y *each*	15·00	9·00
—Z (last series traced to 67Z)	18·00	10·00

B335 **£5**   Multicoloured replacement note

    Prefix coding: Number, number, letter.

Reverse of B334

		Price	
		EF	VF

Quantity printed: 8 million.
Serial letters:
 —M (series traced from 01M to 08M)   40·00   22·00

B336 £5 Multicoloured (pale blue
 predominating)
Prefix coding: Letter, letter, number,
 number.
Quantity printed: 2200 million.
Serial letters:
 AN— (first series traced from AN01)   19·00   10·00
 AR—, AS—, AT—, AU—, AW—,
 AX—, AY—, AZ—
 BN—, BR—, BS—, BT—, BU—,   *each*   15·00   9·00
 BW—, BX—, BY—, BZ—
 CN—, CR—, CS—, CT—, CU—,
 CW—, CX
 EZ—(last series traced to EZ56)   24·00   12·00

1978 (9 February) ONE POUND

Designed by Harry Eccleston as the fourth in the series D (Pictorial) notes.
The obverse has the same portrait of the Queen as used on the £5 note,
and features a medallion of Britannia, a vignette of a design comprising a
caduceus, cornucopia and an olive branch, combined in multicoloured
patterns of green, yellow and blue. On the reverse is a portrait in green of
Sir Issac Newton specially created from a number of contemporary
portraits, together with multicoloured machine-engraved patterns sugges-
ting the solar system, overlaid by a geometric diagram from Newton's
Principia. Printed initially in sheets of 40 by offset, and subsequently in
sheets of 21 on web presses, at the Bank of England Works, Loughton,
Essex, on banknote paper manufactured by Portals Ltd. with watermark
of Newton's head. The notes measure 66·69 × 134·5 mm (2⅝ × 5⁵⁄₁₆ in.)
and are still legal tender. A particular feature of the new £1 note is that
it has only one serial number, printed at the bottom right hand corner.
The top left hand side is left blank for encoding marks which may be used
in future for electronic note-sorting equipment.

B337/340 (common design)

PAGE (contd.)

Reverse of B337/341 (common design). The small letter "W"
denotes web-printed note

	Price	
	EF	*VF*

B337 £1 Multicoloured (green predominating).
Prefix coding: Letter, number, number.
Quantity printed: 1440 million.
Serial letters:

A—(first series traced from A01)   5·00   2·00

B—, C—, D—, E—, H—, J—, K—,
L—, N—, R—, S—, T—, U—, W—, } *each*   4·00   2·00
X—, Y—

Z—(last series traced to Z80)   7·00   2·00

B338 £1 Multicoloured replacement note
Prefix coding: Letter, number, number.
Quantity printed: Probably 1 million.
Serial letters:

M—(series traced in M01 only)   12·00   6·00

Although these notes were prepared as replacements, there is no evidence
they were used for this purpose as the Bank had superceded the "star"
note system as it was called by automatic replacement through Crossfield
counting machines and computerised records.

B339 £1 Multicoloured (green predominating).
Prefix coding: Number, number, letter.
Quantity printed: 1360 million.
Serial letters:

—A (first series traced from 01A)   6·00   2·00

—B, —C, —D, —E, —H, —J, —K,
—L, —N, —R, —S, —T, —U, —W,   *each*
—X, —Y   4·00   2·00

—Z (last series traced in 81Z only)   –   –

It is possible that 81Z which falls outside the usual range of 80 serial
prefixes used by the Bank for £1 notes, is experimental.

		Price	
		EF	*VF*

B340 £1 Multicoloured (green predominating).
Prefix coding: Letter, number, number, letter.
Quantity printed: 475 million.
Serial letters:

		EF	VF
A—N (first series traced from A01N)		5·00	2·00
B—N, C—N, D—N	each	4·00	2·00
E—N (last series traced to E80N)		7·00	2·00

STANLEY GIBBONS SAFE 'N' CLEAR DISPLAY SYSTEM

Stanley Gibbons *Safe 'n' Clear* leaves are ideal for displaying bank notes. The entire system is manufactured only from the highest quality materials guaranteed to give maximum protection. The leaves are of tough matt-black board, colour-fast and completely free of potentially harmful chemicals. The crystal-clear polyester strips contain no softners, acids, solvents or plasticisers and offer substantial protection against ultra-violet radiation, humidity and friction. The bonding between strips and leaf is similarly chemically inert, ensuring that leaves will not warp or buckle under adverse conditions, whilst holding bank notes firmly in place. Leaves are multipunched to fit a vast range of binders from 2 to 22 ring, whatever ring sytem you are using at present, *Safe 'n' Clear* will probably fit it.

There is also a *Safe 'n' Clear Binder* – with a luxuriously padded cover in royal blue and a subtle gold blocked border on the front and spine. It has a four 'D' ring mechanism for easy turning and neat stacking of leaves.

Safe 'n' Clear leaves and binders are available from the Stanley Gibbons shop at 399 Strand, London WC2 or by post from: Stanley Gibbons Publications Ltd, 5 Parkside, Christchurch Rd., Ringwood, Hants, BH24 3SH. Send for our brochure and price list.

Orders may be placed by phone quoting your credit card number – Ringwood (042 54) 2363

David Henry Fitzroy Somerset (1980–)

Born 1930. Entered Bank service 1952. Deputy Chief Cashier 1973. Chief Cashier 1 March 1980.

1981 (20 March) ONE POUND

Design, watermark and dimensions as for J. B. Page series D (Pictorial) notes, but the general appearance is enhanced by the inclusion of additional background colours, mainly lilac, light green, pink and yellow. The Queen's portrait is rather more sharply defined and the portrait of Sir Isaac Newton appears rather more lively. Printed in sheets of 21 on web presses at the Bank of England Works, Loughton, Essex, on banknote paper manufactured by Portals Ltd. The main design on the front is printed by intaglio and the back by offset lithography. The new notes used different serial prefixes and had a small capital "W" on the reverse (standing for Web press).

		Price	
		EF	*VF*
B341 **£1**	Multicoloured (green predominating).		
	Prefix coding: Letter, letter, number, number.		
	Quantity printed: Not yet complete.		
	Serial letters:		
	AN—(first series traced from AN01)	6·00	†
	AR—, AS—, AT—, AU—, AW—,		
	AX—, AY—, AZ—,		
	BN—, BR—, BS—, BT—, BU—,		
	BW—, BX—, BY—, BZ—,		
	CN—, CR—, CS—, CT—, CU—,		
	CW—, CX—, CY—, CZ—,		
	DN—, DR—, DS—, DT—	†	†
	(continuing)		

B341

1980 (June) FIVE POUNDS

Design, dimensions and watermark as for J. B. Page series D (Pictorial) notes. Printed on web presses in sheets of 18 at the Bank of England Works, Loughton, Essex. A small capital "L" on the reverse stands for Litho.

		Price	
		EF	*VF*

B342 **£5** Multicoloured (pale blue
predominating).
Prefix coding: Letter, letter, number,
number.
Quantity printed: Not yet complete.
Serial letters:
DN—(first series traced from DN01) 18·00 †
DR—, DS—, DT—, DU—, DW—,
DX—, DY—, DZ—,
EN—, ER—, ES—, ET—, EU—,
EW—, EX—, EY—, EZ—,
HN—, HR—, HS—, HT—, HU—,
HW—, HX—, HY—, HZ—,
JN—, JR—, JS—, JT—, JU—, JW—,
JX—, JY—,
KN— † †
(*continuing*)

B342/343 (common design)

B343 **£5** Multicoloured experimental notes for
Optical Character Recognition
(OCR).
Prefix coding: Letter, letter, number,
number.
Quantity printed: 9 million.
Serial letters:
AN91, BR91, CS91, DT91, EU91,
HW91, JX91, KY91, LZ91 — —

SOMERSET (contd.)

Five pound notes are prepared in sheets of 18, so that five sheets use up 90 serial numbers. The serial 91 therefore falls outside the normal range. For further details of sheet make-up see page 154.

1980 (December) TEN POUNDS

Design, dimensions and watermark as for J. B. Page series D (Pictorial) notes. Plate-printed in sheets of 20 at the Bank of England Works, Loughton, Essex.

			Price	
			EF	VF
B344 £10	Multicoloured (brown predominating).			
	Prefix coding: Letter, number, number.			
	Quantity printed: 475 million.			
	Serial letters:			
	T—		20·00	†
	U—, W—, X—, Y—	*each*	18·00	†
	Z—(last series traced to Z78)		20·00	†
B345 £10	Multicoloured (brown predominating).			
	Prefix coding: Number, number, letter.			
	Quantity printed: Not yet complete.			
	Serial letters:			
	—A (first series traced from 01A)		20·00	†
	—B, —C, —D, —E, —H, —J, —K		†	†
	(*continuing*)			

B344/346 (common design)

1984 (February) TEN POUNDS

Design, dimensions and watermark as for B344 above, but note carries a small capital letter "L" on the reverse to the right of the £10 denomination, to indicate it was printed by lithography. It is also distinguished by a different serial prefix: Letter, letter, number, number.

	Price	
	EF	*VF*

B346 £10 Multicoloured (brown predominating).
  Prefix coding: Letter, letter, number, number.
  Quantity printed: Not yet complete.
  Serial letters:

AN—(first series traced from AN01	20·00	†
AR—, AS— (*continuing*)	†	†

1981 (date unknown) TWENTY POUNDS

Design, dimensions and watermark as for J. S. Fforde series D (Pictorial) notes. Plate-printed in sheets of 20 at the Bank of England Works, Loughton, Essex.

B347 £20 Multicoloured (purple predominating).
  Prefix coding: Letter, number, number.
  Quantity printed: Not yet complete.
  Serial letters:

E—(first series traced from E01)	40·00	†
(*continuing*)		

1981 (20 March) FIFTY POUNDS

Designed by Harry Eccleston and Roger Withington as the fifth in the series D (Pictorial) notes. The obverse has the same portrait of the Queen as used on the £10 and £20 notes, and features a Phoenix based on a design by Sir Christopher Wren and patterns derived from various design features in St. Paul's Cathedral; a medallion of Britannia completes the picture. On the reverse is a new portrait of Sir Christopher Wren specially created from contemporary portraits by J. B. Closterman (1695) and Sir Godfrey Kneller (1711); the background comprises a view of St. Paul's from the River Thames, a floor plan and a decorative guilloche developed from the wood carvings by Grinling Gibbons in the south choir aisle. Printed in sheets of 15 on banknote paper manufactured by Portals Ltd. with watermark of H.M. The Queen and contoured security thread produced by laser equipment manufactured by the UK Atomic Energy Authority. The notes measure 169 × 95 mm (3¾ × 6⅝ in.).

B348 £50 Multicoloured.
  Prefix coding: Letter, number, number.
  Quantity printed: Not yet complete.
  Serial letters:

A—(first series traced from A01)	85·00	†
B—, C— (*continuing*)	†	†

SOMERSET *(contd.)*

B348

Reverse of B348

Information for the New Collector

Forming a collection

Modern banknotes should be collected in at least EF (extremely fine) condition, and preferably uncirculated. A grading guide will be found on page 160. However, as the hobby expands, this is becoming increasingly difficult as far as earlier notes are concerned, and for nearly all pre-1900 notes it is impossible. Even the better-off collector will probably be happy with a single example of each of the early cashiers between Newland and Nairne—it gets progressively harder after acquiring a Hase £1. Condition becomes of secondary importance to actually tracking down the notes and those of the higher denominations are now thought unlikely to exist in private hands.

From the outbreak of the 1914 war and the progressive expansion of paper money the choice becomes much wider, and although top grade Treasury notes have now become expensive, copies of the lower grades can (with a few exceptions) be acquired for a relatively modest outlay. The same is true of post 1928 Bank of England notes and it is always worth checking present day notes from circulation for an error or an interesting serial number.

There are many ways of forming a collection, ranging through the popular "first and last" of each series, a single example of each type, serial numbers that spell "words" such as COIN, LION, SOIL BOIL, NOI and IOU, specialisation in replacement notes, or a study of errors (which compared with stamps are still remarkably cheap).

When notes are creased or dirty there is a temptation to smarten them up. Some surface marks can be removed easily and safely with a soft india rubber—though not, alas, the curse of the ballpoint pen. Within reason there is no harm in gently washing a modern note in warm water, and then pressing it between the pages of a heavy book. But don't think that you can turn a VF note into an UNC note by this means, and be wary of someone offering overgraded "laundry jobs" at inflated prices. As with every field of collecting it pays to buy the best you can afford from a reputable dealer.

Housing a collection depends to a certain extent on its size and complexity. A wide variety of smartly tiled binders can be found (including those from Stanley Gibbons), but suitable pages are more of a problem. The original floppy vinyl pockets are inexpensive, but even with black card inserts, are not very satisfactory. An alternative is the Gibbons Safe 'n' Clear system, used by philatelists, in which flaps of transparent Melinex polyester are welded to black card—the two strip page is the most commonly used by banknote collectors. A drawback to this method is that notes can be viewed only from one side. Another type of album page, which allows viewing from both sides and uses the same inert Melinex film is marketed by Lindner.

Serial Letters and Numbers

With the exception of the letters I and Q, Treasury notes are found with serial letters from every letter in the alphabet, starting with A and ending with Z.

The Bank of England make a rather more selective use of the alphabet. In the £1 and 10s. issues of C. P. Mahon and B. G. Catterns, all letters of the alphabet were used except for I, P and Q. Later the letters F, G and V were also omitted, giving a conveniently round figure of 20 letters available for each issue. The old white fivers are found with every letter except F, G and Q.

When the portrait notes were introduced in 1960, the letter M was adopted for replacements (as opposed to —A for 10s. and S—S and S—T for £1 notes) and the letter O was dropped. The quantity of notes printed in any given issue has been calculated on the basis of one million for each of the serial prefixes 01–99 (100,000 for white £5 notes). It is by no means certain that each series was completed or if it was actually issued, and it is necessary to check against the notes themselves. The absence of various prefixes and/or numbers in the catalogue merely indicates the extent of the sampling to date—there is no official confirmation from the Bank of England.

Nothing can be "assumed" during the Fforde and Page eras in particular when notes were grouped under a split alphabetical system, combining the first half A to L with the second half N to Z, and then vice versa. Many of these prefixes in the portrait series remain partially or totally unissued.

Replacement Notes

A replacement (or "star" note as it is officially termed) is used by the Bank of England to make up a bundle where one or more notes may have been damaged. At various points in the production run a note from a bundle bearing a different serial prefix from that in progress is inserted. As printing became more complex so the rate of faulty notes increased, but it is still a minute fraction of the total.

Only the Bank can positively identify a replacement note, but although most of the replacement serials are now known, it is sensible with modern issues to preserve the note buttressed where possible on each side by notes from the normal series. This is because replacement serials are known to have been issued in blocks for general circulation, especially at the end of a series or a cashier's term of office.

The "star" note system was discontinued by the Bank in 1981 soon after they had installed high speed Crossfield counting machines. These are programmed to eliminate defective notes marked by yellow felt pens and to make up bundles of the necessary quantity while at the same time recording the serial numbers on a computer for reference. Accordingly notes are no longer necessarily in any particular sequence.

The exception to this system is the £50 denomination, where faulty notes are removed and replaced by hand. Since the numbers of the replacement notes are the same as those removed, they are difficult to identify—as well as expensive to collect!

(*Detailed tables showing the serial numbers of 10s., £1, £5 and £10 notes are given in Appendix A.*)

Britannia replacement serials

Cashier	10s.	£1
K. O. Peppiatt	01A to 03A	S01S to S09S
P. S. Beale	04A to 35A	S10S to S70S
L. K. O'Brien	36A to 68A	S71S to S99S
		S01T to S22T

Portrait replacement serials

Cashier	10s.	£1	£1("G")	£5	£10
L. K. O'Brien	M01 to M18	M01 to M66	—	—	—
J. Q. Hollom	M19 to M53	M68 to M99	—	—	M01
	—	01M to 99M	—	—	—
	—	M01R to M08R	M01N to M28N	M01 to M16	—
J. S. Fforde	M56 to M80	M08R to M49R	M29N to M42N	M17 to M38	M01
	—	R01M to R49M*	N01M to N14M	01M to 15M*	—
	—	S01M to S48M*	—	—	—
	—	T01M to T04M	T29M to T32M	—	—
	—	U01M	—	—	—
J. B. Page	—	R44M to R99M*	—	04M to 14M*	—
		S52M to S95M*	—	—	M01 to M17
		W01M to W81M	—	—	—
		MR01 to MR48	—	—	—
		MS01 to MS84	—	—	—
		MT01 to MT21	—	—	—
		MU01 to MU18	—	—	—
		MW01 to MW19	—	—	—

Pictorial replacement serials

Cashier	£1	£5	£5 ("L")	£10	£20
J. B. Page	M01	M01 to M04	01M to 08M	M01 to M10	M01 to M02

* There is some degree of overlapping on these serials.

Opinion is divided as to the existence of a recognisable replacement system before the Second World War. Nothing has yet come to light to prove or disprove the various serial letters suggested, and the Bank are not prepared to confirm or deny the existence of replacement notes during this period.

In Treasury notes, the most tenable theory on the first issue is that the double letter notes with four serial numbers were used as replacements, but the system does not seem to have extended to later issues. In the third issue the odd letter out is Z, which was used to prefix the bottom right-hand note of each sheet of £1 notes (but not the 10s.). Numerically these are relatively scarce but they may have acted as "control" notes rather than replacements.

Try Finding These Fun Notes		
COIN	OIL	H20
JOIN	OO7	M15
LOIN	O1C	1IN, 2IN, etc.
LION	DO1	1OZ, 2OZ, etc.
BOIL	NO1	11B, 21B, etc.
COIL	IOU	ER02
SOIL	T42	ER25
TOIL	24T	DIOR

and doubtless many more!

Dates

No modern Bank of England notes are dated. Until the introduction of the 10s. and £1 notes in 1928, all notes carried a date and this was maintained on the higher denominations until the last series of white £5 notes in 1956.

Notes were not, however, necessarily issued in the year that they were dated, the most notable examples being those of 1945 (B255) and 1947 (B264). This was because the Bank have always stockpiled notes to ensure sufficient supply for any contingency and to meet extra demand, especially at Christmas.

In 1970, the new £20 note was actually issued after Mr. J. S. Ff orde had ceased to be chief cashier, although it carried his signature. Between the printing and the distribution of the notes he had been promoted and Mr. J. B. Page had become chief cashier.

Specimen Notes

Although Specimen notes are only issued by the Bank of England to other central banks, the number of revolutions and a less meticulous attitude to currency in some parts of the world have lead to quite a number coming on to the market. In the case of Specimen notes from the Portrait series and the Pictorial series, the prefix is invariably A00 000000.

From 1918 to 1960, Specimen notes are scarce, but denominations up to the £1000 have appeared. The earliest white £5 specimen with the signature of E. M. Harvey carries the serial $\frac{001}{Q}$ 00000 and is dated 7 September 1922.

A complete set of high denomination specimens of K. O. Peppiatt from £5 to £1000 was sold at Sotheby's on 22 June 1977. The notes were all dated 20 April 1934 and all carried a Q prefix.

A set of Second World War and post war Peppiatt specimen notes was sold at Stanley Gibbons Auctions in March 1981. The wartime 10s had the prefix Z00D, the £1 A00D and the £5 E00, dated 5 December 1944. The post war 10s. and £1 were prefixed R00 and the £5 L00, dated 24 January 1947.

Most specimen notes are priced in the region £200 to £250, but the higher denominations will be related to their "face" value.

Errors

With the exception of the modern portrait and pictorial notes of Fforde and Page, errors are relatively scarce on Bank of England notes, and on Treasury notes are extremely rare. Because of this it is difficult to put an exact price on every single type of error that may turn up. As a rough guide collectors should expect to pay at least double these prices for Britannia issues and as much as ten times for Treasury note errors. Errors on the modern high denomination notes of £5, £10 and £20 are generally priced at a much lower premium.

For the purpose of quotation the original catalogue number should be cited together with the suffix:

A.   Extra paper, through faulty folding
B.   Serial numbers missing top and bottom
C.   One serial number missing (or partly missing)
D.   Top serial number different from bottom serial
E.   Identical serial numbers on a pair of notes
F.   Identical but different serial numbers top and bottom on a pair of notes (slip'n'stick)
G.   Note printed on one side only
H.   Part of the design omitted
J.   Double or faulty printing (e.g part of the back printed on the front and vice versa)
S.   Specimen

Fforde and Page £1, £5 and £10 notes are found with each cashier's signature on consecutively numbered notes. These will be found listed under the relative issue—they are not errors.

One of the most remarkable errors was the omission of the signature of the Chief Cashier, D. H. F. Somerset from a run of £5 notes in 1981. The serial prefixes affected are between DU55 and DU72, a possible total of 500 sheets or 9000 notes. The actual range of numbers recorded is between 295 and 532, in other words 237 sheets. This would indicate at least 4000 notes escaped, but it is known that many were returned from the clearing banks when the error was noticed.

Error category D: different serial numbers on same note

Error category K: extra paper through faulty folding

Treasury Error Note

Paper and Production

The first Bank of England notes were written by hand on ordinary paper purchased from stationers. Forgery lead the bank at an early stage to experiment with marbled paper which could be matched exactly to a counterfoil and from 1697 watermarked paper was used exclusively.

On 27 November 1724 the Bank signed a contract with Henry Portal of Whitchurch, Hampshire, whose firm became the sole papermaker and remains so to this day. No one else is allowed to use the special Bank watermarked paper, although Portals themselves supply paper to well over 100 other countries for security printing. The Bank holds a 30% stake in the company.

For nearly 100 years note printing was, in fact, in the hands of an outside contractor—until 1748 James Cole, and from 1748 until 1791 George Cole. Each month a supply of paper was sent in large iron-bound chests by wagon to the printers in Great Kirby Street, Hatton Garden. Each morning the engraved copper plates would be drawn from the treasury in the Bank, in Threadneedle Street, and taken to the printing works, where a clerk counted the sheets of notes as they came off the press.

In 1791 Cole's business was transferred to the Bank and from then until 1920 all Bank of England notes were printed on the premises. Despite the decision by Lloyd George to have currency notes issued by the Treasury during the first world war, the Bank's facilities were considerably stretched printing high denomination notes, postal orders (which were legal tender for a few weeks in 1914), divided warrants, military allowance drafts, loan issues, Treasury bills, corporation bills, premium exchequer bonds—well over 500 million documents requiring watermarked paper. The pressure on space at Threadneedle Street was such that in 1916 the Bank purchased St. Luke's Hospital for conversion into a new printing works. Some printing was transferred immediately, but reconstruction did not begin until 1919 and the move was finally completed in April 1922. Thereafter, with the exception of the Second World War emergency issue, all notes were printed at St. Luke's until 1956.

It had become clear some years earlier that a specially designed new printing works would be necessary, and for this purpose the bank purchased a site at Loughton, Essex, in 1951. The new works, occupying half a million square feet of floor space, employs more than 2000 people, of which about 250 are directly involved in note printing. The main printing hall itself stretches some 300 yards. Additional premises were added later for the destruction of notes which had been withdrawn from circulation.

In 1800 a mere 15,000 notes were printed daily; by 1950 there were 939 million printed; by 1960 this figure had jumped to 1627 million and by 1965 to a peak of 2222 (or more than 8½ million a day). Mainly due to the higher denomination notes now in circulation and to a policy of recycling notes, the position has now improved and with a couple of exceptions, the number of new notes printed has stabilised at between 1600 and 1800 million a year.

Number of new notes issued by denomination (millions)

Year to end February	*1975*	*1976*	*1977*	*1978*	*1979*	*1980*	*1981*	*1982*	*1983*	*1984*
£1	1092	1021	985	990	978	969	893	780	728	652
£5	445	482	553	545	509	585	661	644	622	625
£10	55	111	107	133	176	230	247	219	230	451
£20	8	11	16	23	25	35	44	39	34	72
£50	—	—	—	—	—	—	—	6	9	9
	1600	1625	1661	1691	1688	1819	1845	1688	1623	1809

Source: *Bank of England Report and Accounts 1975–1984.*

Notes in Circulation—"A Licence to Print Money"

There are now around 2000 million Bank of England notes in circulation. The £1 note is still the most heavily used denomination and accounts for the largest annual production mainly because of its short life of only nine months. At the time of writing in early 1984, the £1 is scheduled to be phased out in favour of the £1 coin, but adverse publicity about the coin and Parliamentary pressure may cause a change of plan.

The value of £10 notes in circulation now exceeds that of £5 notes. The £10 note which lasts for just under three years, now accounts for 41% of circulation compared with 26% for the £5 note which lasts for about 15 months.

Value of notes in circulation by denominations (£ millions)

End February	1975	1976	1977	1978	1979	1980	1981	1982	1983	1984
£1	884	831	805	800	782	704	673	657	641	583
£5	3014	3261	3431	3625	3694	3540	3343	3097	2850	2554
£10	815	1157	1596	2172	2948	3610	4043	4298	4531	4846
£20	397	500	652	852	1125	1419	1686	1833	1874	1979
£50	—	—	—	—	—	—	—	274	633	909

The total value of notes in circulation includes certain high value notes used internally by the Bank of England and also 10s. notes (last issued in 1969) still outstanding. The figure for 1983 was 12 million 10s. notes, £6 million in value. As a result of the *Currency Act* 1983, which received Royal Assent on 28 March, the Bank is now permitted to write off notes which have not been presented for payment within ten years from the date they ceased to be legal tender from the total of notes issued. Previously this could only be done either 20 or 40 years from the date of issue, depending on the denomination. Series C ten shilling notes, together with Series A, B and C £5 notes and higher value Series A notes were therefore written off in the year to end-February 1984.

Although notes may cease to be legal tender, the Bank's "Promise to Pay the Bearer" is unlimited in time and old notes can always be exchanged for new, although you should always check possible collector interest first.

Much of the work connected with bank-note issue is automated, and a record of the serial numbers of all notes printed is kept by computer. Until 1928 registers were kept not only of how many notes were outstanding but which actual notes they were. These registers are still kept for the old White notes of £10 and higher denominations, which has meant that, given certain guarantees, the Bank could replace lost or stolen notes and replace those badly mutilated. Unpresented notes of the old white high denomination series are written off in the books of the Bank 40 years after their date of issue under the provisions of the Bank Act 1892.

Printing

Until 1960 all notes were plate-printed by the intaglio (recess or line engraved) process. Sheets of paper were fed singly into the machines which then printed a number of notes—24 in the case of the portrait £1. The sheets were then stacked and stored so that the ink could dry before the next stage of printing was undertaken. Several printing processes were needed, and the whole operation took several weeks, before the notes could be finally sorted, counted and packed. It is still used for the £20 and £50 notes.

In the late 1950s, however, the bank assembled a team of engineers and chemists to develop a machine that would print the notes in a single process, from a reel (or "web") of paper into sheets of finished notes. The prototype machine was built by Masson, Scott Thrissell Engineering Ltd., of Bristol, and the first notes, the so-called "R" £1 notes (B283), appeared with the signature of L. K. O'Brien in 1960. Soon afterwards another experimental web press built by the German company, Goebel Darmstad was installed and notes from this machine can be identified by the small capital "G" appearing on the back (see under Hollom and Fforde). Gradually the whole of the production of £1, £5 and £10 notes were transferred to four web presses supplied by Masson, Scott, Thrissell. The reels of paper used are two miles long and this has meant that among other things it has to be especially durable, and the watermark is no longer matched exactly to each note. The machines can print approximately two million £1 notes in a 14-hour day divided into two shifts.

The finished parcels of notes are despatched to the Issue Office of the Bank in London or to one of the seven branches (Birmingham, Bristol, Leeds, Liverpool, Manchester, Newcastle and Southampton) where they are held until required by the clearing banks.

The Bank has kindly supplied the following general information:

Denomina-tion	Sheet size (mm)	Note size (mm)	Notes per sheet	Notes per ream
£1	426·5 × 493·4	134·5 × 66·69	21 (3 × 7)	10,500
£5	459·5 × 493·4	145·5 × 77·8	18 (3 × 6)	9000
£10	621 × 469·35	151 × 84·87	20 (4 × 5)	10,000
£20	657 × 495	160 × 90	20 (4 × 5)	10,000
£50	524 × 518	169 × 95	15 (3 ×5)	7500

Denomina-tion	Notes per packet	Packets per Bundle	Bundles per Parcel	Notes per Parcel	Value
£1	100	5	10	5000	£5000
£5	100	5	10	5000	£25,000
£10	50	5	10	2500	£25,000
£20	50	5	4	1000	£20,000
£50	50	5	4	1000	£50,000

It will be seen from the above information that the numbering limits are: £1—84; £5—90; £10—80; £20—80; £50—90. Each serial prefix consists of 999,999 notes. Notes with the serial number, 1,000,000 used to be done by hand but are no longer issued.

The British public are probably the most fastidious in the world when it comes to the condition of their money. On average 30 notes are printed per head of the population per year with a face value of some £175. In the U.S.A. the figure is about 15 notes and in France 11.

Bank of England Printing Works—£5 notes coming off the Plate Press machine.

*Bank of England Printing Works—General view of the Goebel
machine with machine minder at the Intaglio unit.*

Design

For obvious reasons the main consideration in designing a banknote is security against the forger. Although the design of the Bank of England white notes remained largely unchanged for some 250 years there was a great deal of unobtrusive innovation. The vignette of Britannia was changed at fairly regular intervals, until the definitive version produced by Daniel Maclise, R.A. for the issue of 1855 (illustrated on page 59).

The over-riding concern at all times was to keep one jump ahead of the forgers, and to this end the Bank had a constant stream of designs and suggestions. The Bank Restriction period from 1797 was especially critical and for most of the time a special standing committee was in being to discuss any suitable project. In December 1817 the Bank's attention was drawn to the work of a printer from Croydon called Augustus Applegarth. He and his partner Edward Cowper were working on surface printing in several colours from blocks to be produced by stereotype from an original cut in wood or metal. The committee liked the idea and advanced the sum of £1200 to Applegarth to expedite his designs. During 1818 a Royal Commission was set up to enquire into the mode of preventing forgery of banknotes and the Bank of England were able to report the progress that had been made. In the meantime further sums of money, up to £5000, had been advanced to the Croydon printers.

In February 1819 after receiving several specimens in colour, the Bank's Court of Directors approved one of the Applegarth and Cowper designs. It was planned to introduce the notes, probably in 1820, and an Act of Parliament was passed making it illegal to copy the note which was described thus: "The groundwork of each bank note will be black or coloured, or black or coloured line work, and the words 'Bank of England' will be replaced at the top of each bank note in white letters upon a black, sable or dark ground, such ground containing white lines intersecting each other, and the numerical amount or sum of each bank note in the body of the note will be printed in black and red register work, and the back of each note will distinctly show the whole contents thereof except the number and date in reversed impression".

The Applegarth and Cowper design

By autumn 1821 the Bank had spent a total of £40,000 on developing the new notes, only to find that their own engravers were able to imitate every aspect of the Applegarth and Cowper designs. Thus an interesting, and unique experiment came to an end.

In 1835 the Bank decided to adopt a new system of printing and engraving then in use in Ireland, and the invention of John Oldham. This was in use by 1838 and a committee again started to consider changes in design. In 1839 an elaborate new design was recommended "containing allegorical figures representing Britannia standing on a rock with the shield of the union, the armed prow of a ship and the waves beating at her feet . . . in the centre of the bottom is a medallion containing the heads of King William and Queen Mary as founders of the bank in 1694". This note was not, however, approved by the Court of Directors and, together with other similar allegorical efforts of the 19th century, can only be classified as an unadopted essay.

All work on the current banknotes is undertaken by a department headed until his retirement in 1982 by Mr. Harry Eccleston. His successor is Mr. Roger Withington.

As the *Bank of England Quarterly Bulletin* described the position in a survey (Vol. 18 No. 3, September 1978): "There is no infallible single security feature. Apart from the well-known features such as the water-mark and the thread (invented by Mr. S. B. Chamberlain, General Manager of the bank's printing works, in 1940) the security of a note depends also on the combination of specialised design elements, such as hand-engraved portraits and geometric patterns produced by purpose built machinery, and the use of specialised printing techniques and materials. The artist has to understand and make use of this variety of aids and yet evolve an accept-able design which is fit for mass production . . . the real art is to produce a note such that any attempt at forgery is obvious to a member of the public at a casual glance".

Forgeries and "skit" notes

Over the years many imitations of Bank of England notes have been produced. Some have been merely frivolous "skit" notes, others have had a serious intent, such as George Cruickshank's anti-hanging note aimed at ending the death penalty for passing forged notes. An article entitled "New light on the Cruickshank Anti-hanging note" by Alistair Gibb appeared in *Coin Monthly*, October 1979.

This penalty was applied to innocent and guilty alike following the Act of 1697, although it did not become a serious problem until the early 19th century during the Bank Restriction period. Some 618 people were sentenced to death for forgery in the period 1797–1829, and it wasn't until 1832 that the death sentence was finally abolished and transportation for life was substituted.

It is, even today, an offence for anyone knowingly to purchase, receive from any person, or have in his custody or possession a forged banknote regardless of its age or country of origin. Collectors are advised to famil-iarise themselves with the provisons of the *Forgery and Counterfeiting Act*, 1981 (which superceded the *Forgery Act*, 1913). This states, *inter alia*, that

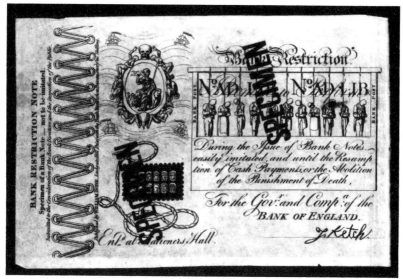

George Cruikshank's note

"It is an offence for any person, unless the relevant authority has previously consented in writing, to reproduce on any substance whatsoever, and whether or not on the correct scale, any British currency note or any part of a British currency note". This clearly covers both photographing and photocopying notes.

Forged notes are immediately confiscated by the Bank of England if presented for verification and this particularly applies to the Second World War forgeries produced by the Nazis at their Sachsenhausen concentration camp. A translation into English of a report on the project by the Czechoslovak Ministry of the Interior was published in 1982 by Jorgen Samod, of Copenhagen. It is available from most banknote dealers.

The safe way to establish that a "white" note is genuine is to take it to the New Issue Office of the Bank of England. There are various tell-tale signs in the German forgeries illustrated in detail in the Czechoslovak Ministry of the Interior report mentioned above. A method of identification, used by many collectors, which appears to be consistently accurate, is as follows:

Look at the triangular toe of the first stroke of the letter "N" in the word "ENgland" in the watermark wording "Bank of England". From the base line of the triangular toe extends a curved line down to the lower edge of the watermark. If that curved line starts slightly to the left of the centre of the base line it is likely to be a genuine note. If the line starts from the centre of the base line the note is almost certainly a German forgery.

How to Grade Condition

Unlike postage stamps, which are usually collected only in perfect condition, banknotes are collectable in various stages of wear and tear. This is because, at times, banknotes were officially cut in half for transport security reasons—the two halves going by separate transport and being joined at the bank of destination; other notes were made to do service for as long as thirty years and none was preserved in uncirculated condition. Rare notes, such as running cash notes, would be acceptable to collectors in very dirty and torn state. This does not, of course, apply to modern banknotes which should be collected in at least VF (very fine) condition.

The new collector can quickly establish the condition of a banknote by using the table below. The basic conditions are:

UNC	uncirculated	100
EF	extremely fine	90
VF	very fine	75
F	fine	55
Fair	fair	30

Some dealers do not distinguish between uncirculated notes which are 100% and those which have been counted by a cashier. This causes a slight bend on one corner and a consequent grading of 98–99%.

Table of Damage Numbers

Cleanliness:

Just detectable soiling	5
Considerable soiling and/or bankers' marks	10
Very dirty note with legibility considerably reduced	20

Folding:

One or two folds that leave only a just-detectable crease	5
Several folds which are clearly visible	10
Many and repeated folds	20

Surface:

Detectable damage to surface	5
Damage to surface at several places or over considerable area	10
Considerable damage to surface over extended areas	20

Edges:

Just detectable roughness or indentation of edges 5
Considerable damage to edges and/or tears not extending beyond
margin of note 10
Badly damaged edges, or tears extending into design of note .. 20

Body:

One or two pin holes 5
Several pin holes, or one or two larger holes 10
Several larger holes 20

As an example let us consider a note which is slightly soiled, has a number
of firm folds, an undamaged surface, slightly damaged edges and a pin hole
or two. the five damage numbers would be:

Cleanliness	5
Folding	10
Surface	0
Edges	5
Body	5
	Total 25

This total is substracted from 100, giving 75, which grades the note as VF
(very fine).

The banknotes in this catalogue have been priced at EF and VF conditions from 1914 and VF before that date.

Bibliography

Very few books have been written about Treasury and Bank of England notes, and those that have are now out of print. The author has found the following useful:

The Currency of the Great War by Benjamin White. Published by Waterlow and Sons, 1921.

Bank of England and Treasury Notes 1694–1970 by D. M. Miller (Minerva Numismatic Handbooks No. 6) published by Corbitt and Hunter Ltd., 1970.

A Guide to Collecting England Banknotes by David Bevan. Published by Larson Publications, 1970.

Money in Britain: A History of the Coins and Notes of the British Isles by C. R. Josset. Published by David and Charles, 1971.

The Bank of England Note by A. D. Mackenzie. Published by the Cambridge University Press, 1953.

The Pound Sterling by A. E. Feaveryear. Published by Oxford University Press, 1931.

Bibliography of the Bank of England by T. A. Stephens. Published by Effingham Wilson & Co, London 1897; Reprinted by Augustus M. Kelley, New York 1968.

A great many histories have been written about the Bank of England itself, including:

The Bank of England From Within by W. Marston Acres. Published by the Oxford University Press, 1931 (two volumes).

The Bank of England: A History by Sir John Clapham. Published by the Cambridge University Press, 1944 (two volumes).

The Bank of England 1891–1944 by R. S. Sayers. Published by The Cambridge University Press, 1976 (two volumes).

Many interesting articles on banknote collecting appear in the quarterly journal of the International Bank Note Society. Full details are obtainable from the Assistant General Secretary:

Suresh K. Gupta
11 Middle Row
North Kensington
London W10 5AT

Appendix A—Serial Numbers of Bank 10s., £1, £5 and £10 Notes

Ten Shillings

The chart lists serial number prefixes grouped by signatory/issue. Columns (left to right) and their entries:

Unthreaded Mahon (LNoNo)
A⁰¹, Z⁰¹, Y—, X—, W—, V—₁₁

Catterns (LNoNo)
V¹⁴, U—, T—, S—, R—, O—, N—, M—, L—, K—₉₉

Peppiatt (LNoNo)
J⁰¹, H—, E—, D—, C—, B—, A—₉₉

Threaded Peppiatt (War)
Z⁰¹ D/E⁰¹, Y— D/E—, X— D/E—₂₁, W—D, U—D, T—D, S—D, R—D, O—D, N—D, M—D, L—D, K—D, J—D, H—D, E—D, D—D, C—D, B—D, A—₉₉ D

Unthreaded Peppiatt (NoNoL)
⁰¹Z, —Y, —X, —W, —U, —T, —S, —R, —O₇₉, ?—N, ?—M, ⁰⁵L — ₇₁
Replacement Notes

Threaded Peppiatt (NoNoL)
₇₂L, —K, —J, —H, —E₉₁, ⁰¹A₀₃

Beale (NoNoL)
⁹³E₃₉, ⁰³D, —C, —B₃₉, ¹⁴A₃₅

Beale (LNoNoL)
Z⁰¹N, Y—N, X—N, W—N, U—N, T—N, S—N, R—N, O—N, N—N, M—N, L—N, K—N, J—N, H—N, E—N, D—N₈₅

O'Brien (NoNoL)
⁸⁶A₆₈
O'Brien (LNoNoL): D⁸⁶Z, C—Z, B—Z, A—₉₅Z

O'Brien (LNoNoL)
Z⁰¹ Y/X⁰¹, Y—Y/X—₁₇, X—Y, W—Y, U—Y, T—Y, S—Y, R—Y, O—Y, N—Y, M—Y, L—Y, K—Y, J—Y, H—Y, E—Y, D—Y, C—Y, B—Y, A—₉₅Y

Portrait O'Brien (LNoNoL)
A⁰¹, B—, C—, D—, E—, H—, J—, K—₆₄, K—₆₅, M⁰¹₁₈, M—₁₉

Hollom (LNoNo)
M—₅₅, N—, R—, S—, T—, U—, W—, X—, Y—, Z—₉₉

Hollom (NoNoL)
⁰¹A, —B, —C, —D, —E, —H, —J, —K, —L
Replacement Notes: —N, ₂₅R

Fforde (NoNoL)
²⁶R, S—, T—, U—, W—, X—, Y—, Z—₉₉

Fforde (LNoNo)
A⁰¹N, B—N, C—N, D—₃₃N
Fforde (LNoNo): M—₈₀⁵⁶

One Pound

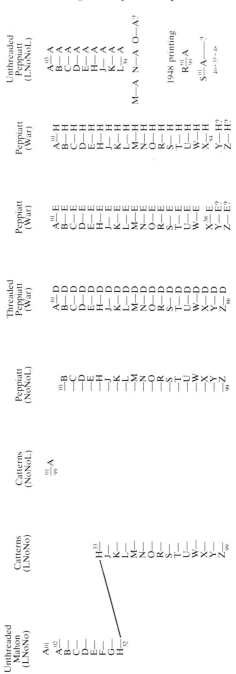

Unthreaded Mahon (LNoNo)	Catterns (LNoNo)	Catterns (NoNoL)	Peppiatt (NoNoL)	Threaded Peppiatt (War)	Peppiatt (War)	Peppiatt (War)	Unthreaded Peppiatt (LNoNoL)
A_{01}		$A\frac{01}{99}$		A^{01}—D	A^{01}—E	A^{01}—H	A^{03}—A
A^{02}			B^{01}	B—D	B—E	B—H	B—A
B—			C—	C—D	C—E	C—H	C—A
C—			D—	D—D	D—E	D—H	D—A
D—			E—	E—D	E—E	E—H	E—A
E—			H—	H—D	H—E	H—H	H—A
F—			J—	J—D	J—E	J—H	J—A
G—	H^{33}		K—	K—D	K—E	K—H	K—A
$H\frac{}{32}$	J—		L—	L—D	L—E	L—H	$L\frac{}{39}$—A
	K—		M—	M—D	M—E	M—H	
	L—		N—	N—D	N—E	N—H	
	M—		O—	O—D	O—E	O—H	M—A N—A O—A?
	N—		R—	R—D	R—E	R—H	
	O—		S—	S—D	S—E	S—H	**1948 printing**
	R—		T—	T—D	T—E	T—H	$R\frac{01}{99}$—A
	S—		U—	U—D	U—E	U—H	S^{11}—A——?
	T—		W—	W—D	W—E	W—H	40—55—48
	U—		X—	X—D	X^{28}—E	X^{94}—H	
	W—		Y—	Y—D	Y—E?	Y—H?	
	X—		$Z\frac{}{99}$	Z_{86}—D	Z—E?	Z—H?	
	Y—						
	$Z\frac{}{99}$						

One Pound *(continued)*

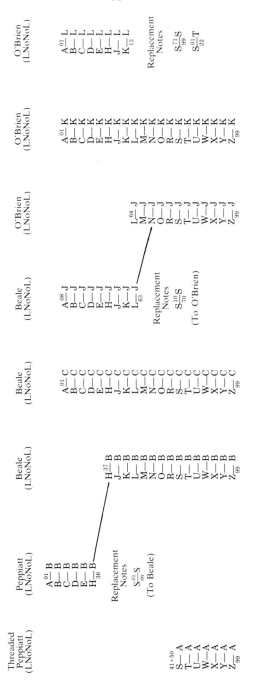

Threaded Peppiatt (LNoNoL)

41+50
S—A
T—A
U—A
W—A
X—A
Y—A
Z_{99}—A

Peppiatt (LNoNoL)

A^{01}—B
B—B
C—B
D—B
E—B
H_{36}—B

Replacement Notes
S^{11}_{19}—S
(To Beale)

Beale (LNoNoL)

H^{37}—B
J—B
K—B
L—B
M—B
N—B
O—B
R—B
S—B
T—B
U—B
W—B
X—B
Y—B
Z_{99}—B

Beale (LNoNoL)

A^{01}—C
B—C
C—C
D—C
E—C
H—C
J—C
K—C
L—C
M—C
N—C
O—C
R—C
S—C
T—C
U—C
W—C
X—C
Y—C
Z_{99}—C

Beale (LNoNoL)

A^{08}—J
B—J
C—J
D—J
E—J
H—J
J—J
K—J
L_{63}—J

Replacement Notes
S^{10}_{70}—S
(To O'Brien)

O'Brien (LNoNoL)

L^{64}—J
M—J
N—J
O—J
R—J
S—J
T—J
U—J
W—J
X—J
Y—J
Z_{99}—J

O'Brien (LNoNoL)

A^{01}—K
B—K
C—K
D—K
E—K
H—K
J—K
K—K
L—K
M—K
N—K
O—K
R—K
S—K
T—K
U—K
W—K
X—K
Y—K
Z_{99}—K

O'Brien (LNoNoL)

A^{01}—L
B—L
C—L
D—L
E—L
H—L
J—L
K_{13}—L

Replacement Notes
S^{71}_{99}—S
S^{01}_{22}—T

One Pound (continued)

Portrait O'Brien (LNoNo)	O'Brien (NoNoL)	O'Brien (LNoNoL)	Hollom (LNoNoL)	Hollom (LNoNoL)	Hollom (LNoNoL)	Hollom (LNoNoL)
A^{01}—	^{01}A	$A^{01}_{06}N^{R}$	$A^{09}_{77}N^{G}$	A—S	A—U	A—X
B—	—B	$B^{01}_{77}N$	B—N	B—S	B—U	B—X
C—	—C	Replacements Hollom (LNoNo)	C—N	C—S	C—U	C—X
D—	—D	M^{68}_{99}	D—N	D—S	D—U	D—X
E—	—E	Hollom (NoNoL)	E—N	E—S	E—U	E—X
H—	—H	$^{01}_{99}M$	H—N	H—S	H—U	H—X
J—	—J		J—N	J—S	J—U	J—X
K—	—K		K—N	K—S	K—U	K—X
L—	—L		L—N	L—S	L—U	$L—X^{G}$
M^{01}_{68}	Replacements		$M^{01}_{08}N_{G}$	$M^{01}_{08}R$	Links to Fforde	A—Y
N—	—N		A—R	A—T	A—W	B_{11}—Y
R—	—R		B—R	B—T	B—W	Link to Fforde
S—	—S		C—R	C—T	$C—W^{G}$	
T—	—T		D—R	$D—T^{G}$	D—W	
U—	—U		E—R	E—T	E—W	
W—	—W		H—R	H—T	H—W	
X—	—Y		J—R	J—T	J—W	
Y—	$—Z_{99}$		K—R	K—T	K—W	
Z_{99}			L—R	L—T	L—W	

One Pound (continued)

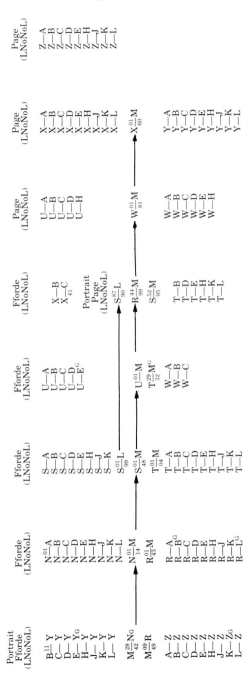

One Pound *(continued)*

Portrait Page (LLNoNo)	Page (LLNoNo)	Page (LLNoNo)	Newton Page (LNoNo)	Page (NoNoL)	Page (LNoNoL)	Newton Somerset (LLNoNo)	Somerset (LLNoNo)
AN^{01}	CN—	EN—	A^{01}	^{01}A	A^{01}N	AN^{01}	CN—
AR—	CR—	ER—	B—	—B	B—N	AR—	CR—
AS—	CS—	ES—	C—	—C	C—N	AS—	CS—
AT—	CT—	ET—	D—	—D	D—N	AT—	CT—
AU—	CU—	EU—	E—	—E	E—N$_{80}$	AU—	CU—
AW—	CW—	EW—	H—	—H		AW—	CW—
AX—	CX—	EX—	J—	—J		AX—	CX—
AY—	CY—	EY—	K—	—K		AY—	CY—
AZ—	CZ—	EZ—	L—	—L		AZ—	CZ—
MR$^{01}_{48}$	MT$^{01}_{21}$	MW$^{01}_{19}$	M^{01} (only)	Replacements			
MS$^{01}_{84}$	MU$^{01}_{18}$	HN—	N—	—N		BN—	DN—
BN—	DN—	HR—	R—	—R		BR—	DR—
BR—	DR—	HS—	S—	—S		BS—	DS—
BS—	DS—	HT—	T—	—T		BT—	DT—
BT—	DT—	HU—	U—	—U		BU—	*(continuing)*
BU—	DU—	HW—	W—	—W		BW—	
BW—	DW—	HX—	X—	—X		BX—	
BX—	DX—	HY—	Y—	—Y		BY—	
BY—	DY—	HZ$_{62}$	Z$_{80}$	^{81}Z (only)		BZ—	
BZ—	DZ—						

Five Pounds

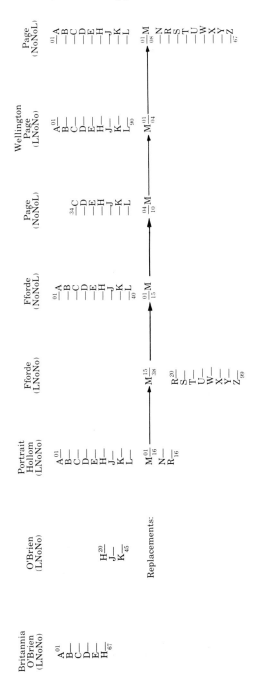

Britannia O'Brien (LNoNo)	O'Brien (LNoNo)	Portrait Hollom (LNoNo)	Fforde (LNoNo)	Fforde (NoNoL)	Page (NoNoL)	Wellington Page (LNoNo)	Page (NoNoL)
A[01]		A[01]		A[01]		A[01]	A[01]
B—		B—		B—		B—	B—
C—		C—		C—	C[34]	C—	C—
D—		D—		D—	D—	D—	D—
E—		E—		E—	E—	E—	E—
H[67]	H[20]	H—		H—	H—	H—	H—
	J—	J—		J—	J—	J—	J—
	K[45]	K—		K—	K—	K—	K—
		L—		L[40]	L—	L[90]	L—
			M[15][38]	M[01][15]	M[04][10]	M[01][04]	M[01][08]
		N—	R[20]				N—
		R[16]	S—				R—
			T—				S—
			U—				T—
			W—				U—
			X—				W—
			Y—				X—
			Z[99]				Y—
							Z[65]

Replacements:

Ten Pounds

Portrait Hollom (LNoNo)	Nightingale Page (LNoNo)	Somerset (LNoNo)	Somerset (NoNoL)
A^{01}_{40}	A^{01}		^{01}A
?M01	B—		—B
	C—		—C
Fforde (LNoNo)	D—		—D
A^{41}_{95}	E—		—E
M01 (only)	H—		—H
	J—		—J
Page (LNoNo)	K—		—K
A^{92}	L—		
B—	N—		**Somerset (LLNoNo)**
C—	R—	?T—	AN—
D—	S—	U—	AR—
E—	T_{20}	W—	AS—
M^{01}_{14}		X—	
		Y—	
		Z_{58}	

Five Pounds (continued)

Wellington Page (LLNoNo)	Page (LLNoNo)	Somerset (LLNoNo)	Somerset (LLNoNo)
AN01	CN—	DN01	HN—
AR—	CR—	DR—	HR—
AS—	CS—	DS—	HS—
AT—	CT—	DT—	HT—
AU—	CU—	DU—	HU—
AW—	CW—	DW—	HW—
AX—	CX_{36}	DX—	HX—
AY—		DY—	HY—
AZ—		DZ—	HZ—
BN—		EN—	JN—
BR—		ER—	JR—
BS—		ES—	JS—
BT—		ET—	JT—
BU—		EU—	JU—
BW—		EW—	JW—
BX—		EX—	JX—
BY—		EY—	JY—
BZ—		EZ^{57}_{90}	*(continuing)*
	EZ^{52}_{56}		

Notes number 91 are experimental (see under B)

Appendix B—Key to the White High Denomination Notes

Prefixes

Thanks to the work of fellow collector Howard Lunn (based on earlier research by Ernest Quarmby and Jim Coulthard) the mystery of the white high denomination notes has finally been unravelled.

Mr. Lunn discovered that it was possible to find out the prefix or date of any of these Bank of England notes by using the following formula:

1. Eliminate each Sunday in the year; also Christmas Day and Good Friday.
2. Distinguish between those years ending with even numbers and those ending with odd numbers.
3. In even years count the numbering only as far as the 17th; in odd years count the numbering from the 18th day.

The system does, in fact, have certain unexplained gaps, but with sufficient sampling of actual notes it has been possible to put together a complete £5 chart starting from 5th May 1920 when the prefix $\frac{A}{1}$ was used, right up until the end of the series in 1956.

Moreover it can also be seen how the branch notes fit into the pattern and how the notes from £10 to £1000 are allocated certain special serial combinations of their own.

Watermarks

The watermarks in Bank of England white notes also vary according to a formula, which includes the year of issue, of printing or of paper manufacture. For the period 1920–1944, the watermark consists of four figures. The last two numbers refer to the year and the first two refer to a particular week (from 01 to 52). Whether this is the week that the notes were printed or the week in which the paper was manufactured is not clear. Possibly it is neither, and it is certainly not the week in which the notes are dated.

A similar problem arises in unravelling the system used by the Bank when they changed the watermark to head off the Nazi forgeries in 1944. Starting with the serial prefix E01 (signed by Peppiatt) in September 1944, a five figure watermark was used. The first four figures now remained the same for a lengthy period and referred to the year but the last figure changed and, as research by Mr. Ian Frazer and others has shown, recurred every eighth working day (See *IBNS Journal*, Vol. 23 No. 2, 1984).

So, for example, it can be seen that the O'Brien LNoNoL series A—A starts with the watermark 19551(A01A) and continues with 19552(A02A),

19553(A03A) and so on with the watermark 19551 recurring at A09A, A17A through to A97A. A99A would be watermarked 19552 and B01A presumably 19553.

The presumption is that 1955 continued to be used on O'Brien notes until the end of the year, but this is by no means certain as the year in the watermark does not necessarily tally with the year of issue. This can be seen from a random study of Beale £5 notes which show the year watermark as 1952 on a note issued in August 1950 (S24) and 1955 on a note issued in June 1952 (X99). Moreover it is not easy to explain the discrepancy as date of paper manufacture or date of printing when that discrepancy is as much as three years after the date of issue.

All one can say with certainty is that the Bank left nothing to chance in building up their formidable defences against forgery, and the watermark system undoubtedly contributed to that end.

E. M. Harvey $\dfrac{A}{1}$ (6 May 1920)   to $\dfrac{A}{99}$ (1 December 1920)

$\dfrac{B}{01}$ (2 December 1920) to $\dfrac{B}{99}$ (24 August 1921)

$\dfrac{C}{01}$ (25 August 1921)   to $\dfrac{C}{99}$ (6 April 1922)

$\dfrac{D}{01}$ (7 April 1922)   to $\dfrac{D}{73}$ (6 September 1922)

$\dfrac{101}{D}$ (7 September 1922) to $\dfrac{399}{D}$ (11 August 1924)

$\dfrac{001}{E}$ (12 August 1924)   to $\dfrac{98}{E}$ (31 March 1925)

C. P. Mahon: $\dfrac{99}{E}$ (18 April 1925)   to $\dfrac{399}{E}$ (19 March 1927)

$\dfrac{001}{H}$ (21 March 1927)   to $\dfrac{197}{H}$ (4 August 1928)

B. G. Catterns: $\dfrac{198}{H}$ (27 March 1929)   to $\dfrac{399}{H}$ (7 July 1930)

$$\frac{001}{J}\text{(9 July 1930)} \qquad \text{to} \quad \frac{399}{J}\text{(6 August 1934)}$$

K. O. Peppiatt: $\frac{352}{J}$ (1 May 1934) $\qquad$ to $\quad \frac{432}{J}$ (10 October 1934)
(1934–44)

$$\frac{A}{101}\text{(11 October 1934)} \quad \text{to} \quad \frac{A}{399}\text{(18 May 1937)}$$

$$\frac{B}{101}\text{(19 May 1937)} \qquad \text{to} \quad \frac{B}{399}\text{(7 November 1940)}$$

$$\frac{C}{101}\text{(8 November 1940)} \quad \text{to} \quad \frac{C}{399}\text{(11 May 1943)}$$

$$\frac{D}{001}\text{(12 May 1943)} \qquad \text{to} \quad \frac{D}{318}\text{(1 September 1944)}$$

K. O. Peppiatt: E01 (2 September 1944) to E99 (27 December 1944)
(1944–45)   H01 (28 December 1944) to H99 (23 April 1945)
Thick paper   J01 (24 April 1945) to J99 (16 August 1945)
                 K01 (17 August 1945) to K99 (10 December 1945)
                 L01 (11 December 1945) to L02 (12 December 1945)

K. O. Peppiatt: L03 (1 January 1947) to L99 (24 April 1947)
(1947   M01 (25 April 1947) to M71 (16 July 1947)
Thin paper

C. S. Beale: M 72 (1 March 1949) to M99 (1 April 1949)
                 N01 (2 April 1949) to N99 (27 July 1949)
                 001 (28 July 1949) to O09 (19 November 1949)
                 P01 (21 November 1949) to P99 (15 March 1950)
                 R01 (16 March 1950) to R99 (10 July 1950)
                 S01 (11 July 1950) to S99 (2 November 1950)
                 T01 (3 November 1950) to T99 (27 February 1951)
                 U01 (28 February 1951) to U99 (23 June 1951)
                 V01 (24 June 1951) to V99 (17 October 1951)
                 W01 (18 October 1951) to W99 (11 February 1952)
                 X01 (12 February 1952) to X99 (6 June 1952)
                 Y01 (7 June 1952) to Y70 (27 August 1952)

L. K. O'Brien: Y71 (17 January 1955) to Y99 (18 February 1955)
Z01 (19 February 1955) to Z99 (15 June 1955)
A01A (16 June 1955) to A99A (8 October 1955)
B01A (10 October 1955) to B99A (2 February 1956)
C01A (3 February 1956) to C99A (28 May 1956)
D01A (29 May 1956) to D99A (20 September 1956)

The London £5 note serials used the letters A to J; K and L prefixed London £10 notes; M was used for London £20; N for the £50; O for the £100; R for the £500; and S for the £1000 notes which were only issued in London.

The branch note serials picked up with T and U for £5 notes; V for £10; W for £20; X for £50; Y for £100 and Z for the £500 denomination. Thus the alphabet was neatly rounded off. All branch notes were called in at the outbreak of war in September 1939. The last dates of issue were in 1938.

£5 Branch:

$$\frac{01}{T} \text{ to } \frac{99}{T} \text{ (1912 to 1916)} \qquad \frac{01}{U} \text{ to } \frac{99}{U} \text{ (1916 to 1919)}$$

$$\frac{T}{01} \text{ to } \frac{T}{99} \text{ (1919 to 1921)} \qquad \frac{U}{01} \text{ to } \frac{U}{99} \text{ (1921 to 1922)}$$

$$\frac{101}{U} \text{ to } \frac{483}{U} \text{ (1921 to 1931)} \qquad \frac{T}{101} \text{ to } \frac{T}{280} \text{ (1931 to 1938)}$$

£10 London:

£10 Branch:

$$\frac{01}{K} \text{ to } \frac{99}{K} \text{ (1914 to 1920)} \qquad \frac{28}{V} \text{ to } \frac{170}{V} \text{ (1918 to 1938)}$$

$$\frac{01}{L} \text{ to } \frac{199}{L} \text{ (1921 to 1931)}$$

$$\frac{K}{101} \text{ to } \frac{K}{199} \text{ (1932 to 1938)}$$

$$\frac{L}{101} \text{ to } \frac{L}{138} \text{ (1938 to 1942)}$$

£20 London:
$$\frac{17}{M} \text{ to } \frac{57}{M} \text{ (1918 to 1938)}$$

£20 Branch:
$$\frac{17}{W} \text{ to } \frac{62}{W} \text{ (1918 to 1937)}$$

£50 London:
$$\frac{11}{N} \text{ to } \frac{66}{N} \text{ (1918 to 1940)}$$

£50 Branch:
$$\frac{43}{X} \text{ to } \frac{76}{X} \text{ (1925 to 1934)}$$

£100 London:
$$\frac{15}{O} \text{ to } \frac{58}{O} \text{ (1919 to 1938)}$$

£100 Branch:
$$\frac{77}{Y} \text{ to } \frac{96}{Y} \text{ (1933 to 1936)}$$
$$\frac{Y}{05} \text{ (1937)}$$

£500 London:
$$\frac{05}{R} \text{ (1925)}$$

£500 Branch:
$$\frac{43}{Z} \text{ (1936)}$$

£1000 London:
$$\frac{05}{S} \text{ to } \frac{14}{S} \text{ (1925 to 1938)}$$

STANLEY GIBBONS SAFE 'N' CLEAR DISPLAY SYSTEM

Stanley Gibbons *Safe 'n' Clear* leaves are ideal for displaying bank notes. The entire system is manufactured only from the highest quality materials guaranteed to give maximum protection. The leaves are of tough matt-black board, colour-fast and completely free of potentially harmful chemicals. The crystal-clear polyester strips contain no softners, acids, solvents or plasticisers and offer substantial protection against ultra-violet radiation, humidity and friction. The bonding between strips and leaf is similarly chemically inert, ensuring that leaves will not warp or buckle under adverse conditions, whilst holding bank notes firmly in place. Leaves are multipunched to fit a vast range of binders from 2 to 22 ring, whatever ring sytem you are using at present, *Safe 'n' Clear* will probably fit it.

There is also a *Safe 'n' Clear Binder* – with a luxuriously padded cover in royal blue and a subtle gold blocked border on the front and spine. It has a four 'D' ring mechanism for easy turning and neat stacking of leaves.

Safe 'n' Clear leaves and binders are available from the Stanley Gibbons shop at 399 Strand, London WC2 or by post from: Stanley Gibbons Publications Ltd, 5 Parkside, Christchurch Rd., Ringwood, Hants, BH24 3SH. Send for our brochure and price list.

Orders may be placed by phone quoting your credit card number – Ringwood (042 54) 2363

Appendix C—Inventory of dies and plates of the Treasury Note Issue handed over to the Bank of England

Although production of Treasury notes had ceased in 1928 the third issue remained legal tender until 1 August 1933. In 1932 consideration was given to what should happen to the working plates, drawings, paper moulds etc. used in production. It was decided to destroy most of this material "with the exception for the purposes of record and history, of a complete set as far as possible of materials (including the original dies etc.) used for each type of note printed, together with a few experimental designs" (Director of Stamping memorandum 27 April 1932).

This material was subsequently offered to, and accepted by the Bank of England for safe keeping, although they were not interested in the experimental designs and these were apparently destroyed. An accumulation of forged notes was also destroyed, though a specimen of each type was kept for record purposes.

Acknowledgement of the safe receipt of the material was sent by the General Works Manager (Mr. Chamberlain) on 17 February 1933, the items are set out in detail in the list below:

Exhibits

Consecutive number	Die, plate, drawing etc.	Description
		1s. Currency notes
1	Original die	King's head—also used for 2s.6d. value
2	Original die	Signature "N. F. Warren Fisher"
3	Original plate	Front of note—without border and scroll
4	Original plate	Border and scroll
5	Original plate	Back of note
		2s. 6d. Currency notes
6	Original die	Signature "N. F. Warren Fisher"
7	Original plate	Front of note—without border and scroll
8	Original plate	Border and scroll

Consecutive number	Die, plate, drawing etc.	Description
9	Original plate	Back of note
		5s. Currency notes
10	Original Drawing	Photogravure section of note
11	Original plate	Portion of scroll for colour overprint for front of note
11A	Original plate	Remaining portion of scroll for colour overprint for front of note
12	Working original electrotype	Overprint—made from 11 and 11A (with medallion of King's head)
13	Working original electrotype	Scroll to complete colour overprint—made from 11 and 11A
14	Original plate	Signature "N. F. Warren Fisher"
15	Original plate	Wording and signature—front of note
16	Original plate	Back of note
		10s. Currency notes—1st issue
17	Original die	King's head—two engravings on one plate—also used for the £1 value (first issue)
18	Original plate (2 set)	Note
19	Original plate	Note
20	Original plate	Note—mounted for electrotyping
		10s. Currency notes—2nd issue
21	Original die	King's head—also used for £1 value (second issue)
22	Original plate	Note
		10s. Currency notes—3rd issue
23	Original Drawing	Photogravure section of note. This drawing was used in conjunction with the original drawing No. 38
24	Original plate	Medallion and bar for overprint
25	Original plate	Scroll overprint to complete bar
26	Original plate	Wording on front and signature "John Bradbury"
27	Original plate	Two signatures "N. F. Warren Fisher"—one for 10s. value and one for £1 value
28	Original plate	Back of note
29	Original plate	Two headings showing alteration to *Northern Ireland*—one for 10s. value and one for £1 value

Consecutive number	Die, plate, drawing etc.	Description
		£1 Currency notes—1st issue
30	Original Drawing	Note
31	Original plate (2 set)	Note
32	Original plate (2 set)	Note
		£1 Currency notes—2nd issue
33	Original plate	Note
		£1 Currency notes—3rd issue
34	Photograph	Sir B. Mackennall's plaster cast of St. George and Dragon
35	Steel plate	St. George and Dragon
36	Copper plate	St. George and Dragon
37	Print	Proof of copper plate No. 36
38	Original Drawing	Photogravure section of note
39	Original plate	Medallion and bar for overprint
40	Original plate	Scroll overprint to complete bar
41	Original plate	Wording on front and signature "John Bradbury"
42	Original plate	Back of note

Appendix D—Draft Bills to Authorise the Issue of 5s. Currency Notes, 1918

Authorise the issue of Currency Notes for five shillings and to enable His Majesty by proclamation to declare Postal Orders to be legal tender.

Be it enacted by the King's most Excellent Majesty, by and with the advice and consent of the Lords Spiritual and Temporal, and Commons, in this present Parliament assembled, and by the authority of the same, as follow:—

1.—(1) The Treasury may, subject to the provisions of this Act, issue currency notes for five shillings, and those notes shall be current in the United Kingdom in the same manner and to the same extent and as fully as silver coin is current, and shall be legal tender in the United Kingdom for the payment of an amount not exceeding forty shillings, but for no greater amount.

(2) Currency notes under this Act shall be in such form and of such design and printed from such plate and on such paper and be authenticated in such manner as may be directed by the Treasury.

(3) The holder of a currency note under this Act shall be entitled to obtain on demand, during office hours at the Bank of England, payment for the note at its face value in such manner as is herein-after provided.

(4) The Treasury may, subject to such conditions as to time, manner and order of presentation as they think fit, call in any currency notes under this Act on paying for those notes at their face value in such manner as is hereinafter provided, or on exchanging those notes for other notes of the same face value issued under this Act, or for notes issued under the Currency and Bank Notes Act, 1914.

(5) Any payment to be made under the foregoing provisions of this section for any currency notes shall be made, as the Treasury think fit, either wholly in silver coin which is for the time being legal tender in the United Kingdom, or where two or more notes are presented for payment together by any person either wholly in gold coin which is for the time being legal tender in the United Kingdom, or partly in such gold coin and partly in such silver coin.

(6) Currency notes under this Act shall be deemed to be bank notes within the meaning of the Forgery Act, 1913, and any other enactment

relating to offences in respect of bank notes which is for the time being in force in any part of the British Islands, and to be valuable securities within the meaning of the Larceny Act, 1861, the Larceny Act, 1916, and any other law relating to stealing which is for the time being in force in any part of the British Islands, and to be current coin of the realm for the purpose of the Acts relating to truck and any other like enactment.

2. Currency notes may be issued to such persons and in such manner as the Treasury direct, but the amount of any notes issued to any person shall, by virtue of this Act and without registration or further assurance be a floating charge in priority to all other floating charges, whether under statute or otherwise, on the assets of that person.

Alternative for Clauses 1 and 2

1. The provisions of the Currency and Bank Notes Act, 1914, as amended by the Currency and Bank Notes (Amendment) Act, 1914, and section twenty-seven of the Finance Act, 1915, shall be extended so as to authorise the issue of currency notes for five shillings, and those Acts shall, subject as hereinafter provided, have effect as if the reference in the Currency and Bank Notes Act, 1914, to currency notes for one pound and ten shillings included a reference to currency notes for five shillings, and as if the references in any of those Acts to currency notes under the Currency and Bank Notes Act, 1914, included references to currency notes under that Act as amended by this Act.

DRAFT

OF A

BILL

TO

Amend the Currency and Bank Notes Act, 1914, so as to authorise the issue of Currency Notes for five shillings and enable His Majesty by proclamation to declare Postal Orders to be legal tender.

Be it enacted by the King's most Excellent Majesty, by and with the advice and consent of the Lords Spiritual and Temporal, and Commons, in this present Parliament assembled, and by the authority of the same, as follows:—

1.—The provisions of the Currency and Bank Notes Act, 1914, as amended by the Currency and Bank Notes (Amendment) Act, 1914, and section twenty-seven of the Finance Act, 1915, shall be extended so as to authorise the issue of currency notes for five shillings, and those enactments shall, subject as hereinafter provided, have effect as if the reference in the Currency and Bank Notes Act, 1914, to currency notes for one pound and ten shillings included a reference to currency notes for five shillings, and as if the references in any of those enactments to currency notes under the Currency and Bank Notes Act, 1914, included references to currency notes under that Act as amended by this Act:

Provided that—

    (*a*) Currency notes for five shillings shall be current only in the same manner and to the same extent as silver coins, and shall be legal tender only for the payment of an amount not exceeding forty shilings; and

(b) Payment for currency notes for five shillings shall not be required to be made in gold coin, but shall be made, as the Treasury think fit, either wholly in silver coin which is for the time being legal tender in the United Kingdom, or where two or more notes are presented for payment together by any person either wholly in gold coin which is for the time being legal tender in the United Kingdom or partly in such gold coin and partly in such silver coin.

2.—(1) His Majesty may by proclamation declare that any postal orders, whether issued before or, after the date of the proclamation, shall be current in the United Kingdom in the same manner and to the same extent and as fully as silver coins are current, and shall be legal tender in the United Kingdom for the payment of an amount not exceeding forty shillings but for no greater amount.

(2) While any such proclamation as aforesaid is in force the holder of any postal order shall be entitled to obtain on demand, during office hours at the Bank of England, payment for the postal order at its face value in any coin which is for the time being legal tender in the United Kingdom for the amount of the order, and the operation of provisoes (b) and (c) to subsection (1) of section twenty-four of the Post Office Act, 1908, shall be suspended.

(3) Any proclamation made under this section may, without prejudice to the making of a new proclamation, be at any time revoked by His Majesty by proclamation, and any proclamation revoking a proclamation declaring postal orders to be legal tender may provide for the calling in or exchange of any postal orders affected thereby.

3.—(1) This Act may be cited as the Currency and Bank Notes (Amendment) Act, 1918, and the Currency and Bank Notes Act, 1914, the Currency and Bank Notes (Amendment) Act, 1914, and this Act may be cited together as the Currency and Bank Notes Acts, 1914 to 1918.

(2) This Act shall apply to the Isle of Man as if it were part of the United Kingdom, but shall not apply to any other British possession.

Provided that—

(a) Currency notes for five shillings shall be current only in the same manner and to the same extent as silver coins, and shall be legal tender only for the payment of an amount not exceeding forty shillings; and

(b) Payment for currency notes for five shillings shall not be required to be made in gold coin, but shall be made, as the Treasury think fit, either wholly in silver coin which is for the time being legal tender in the United Kingdom, or where two or more notes are presented for payment together by any person either wholly in gold coin which is for the time being legal tender in the United Kingdom or partly in such gold coin and partly in such silver coin.

3.—(1) His Majesty may by proclamation declare that any postal orders, whether issued before or after the date of the proclamation, shall be current and legal tender in the United Kingdom in the same manner and to the same extent and as fully as current coins, and shall be legal tender in the United Kingdom for the payment of any amount.

(2) While any such proclamation as aforesaid is in force the holder of any postal order shall be entitled to obtain on demand, during office hours at the Bank of England, payment for the postal order at its face value in any coin which is for the time being legal tender in the United Kingdom for the amount of the order, and the operation of provisoes (*b*) and (*c*) to sub-section (1) of section twenty-four of the Post Office Act, 1908, shall be suspended.

(3) Any proclamation made under this section may, without prejudice to the making of a new proclamation, be at any time revoked by His Majesty by proclamation, and any proclamation revoking a proclamation declaring postal orders to be legal tender may provide for the calling in or exchange of any postal orders affected thereby.

4.—(1) This Act may be cited as the Currency Act, 1918.

(2) This Act shall apply to the Isle of Man as if it were part of the United Kingdom, but shall not apply to any other British possession.